Moodle Gradebook

Second Edition

Explore the Moodle Gradebook and discover how to set up and customize it to track students' progress

Rebecca Barrington

[PACKT] PUBLISHING

open source*
community experience distilled

BIRMINGHAM - MUMBAI

Moodle Gradebook

Second Edition

First published: April 2012

Second edition: December 2014

Production reference: 1121214

Published by Packt Publishing Ltd.
Livery Place
35 Livery Street
Birmingham B3 2PB, UK.

ISBN 978-1-78439-937-5

www.packtpub.com

Credits

Author
Rebecca Barrington

Reviewers
David Le Blanc

Belinda Caulfield

Ann Morgan

Commissioning Editor
Dipika Gaonkar

Acquisition Editor
Sam Wood

Content Development Editor
Anand Singh

Technical Editor
Mohita Vyas

Copy Editors
Vikrant Phadkay

Stuti Srivastava

Project Coordinator
Akash Poojary

Proofreaders
Simran Bhogal

Maria Gould

Ameesha Green

Indexer
Tejal Soni

Production Coordinator
Manu Joseph

Cover Work
Manu Joseph

About the Author

Rebecca Barrington has been using Moodle for over 9 years while working at South Devon College. She provides a range of support, training, and information guides for teaching staff and uses Moodle in her own teaching. She has a keen interest in using technology to support learning and is continually developing new ways of using Moodle and applying them to the development of online courses for use by students.

South Devon College has a reputation for their use of technology, and Rebecca has travelled around the UK to deliver training and advice on using Moodle to other organizations as well as at regional and national events. She has delivered presentations on Moodle at a number of UK MoodleMoots and was a keynote speaker at the iMoot 2013. She is also a regular contributor to online VLE forums where she shares ideas and advice.

Rebecca can be found online via Twitter at @bbarrington.

I would like to thank my family and friends, in particular Marilyn, Dave, Maria, and Rob, for giving me the free time to write and for checking that the information made sense to non-Moodlers! I would also like to thank Bayley, Madeline, Emilie, and Ava for allowing me to use their names (and their parents who gave their consent) so that we had some students to apply the grades to.

I would like to thank South Devon College for allowing me to write this book and the teaching staff who are using the Gradebook to track grades and progress to support our students. Thank you for putting the instructions into real-life practice and for helping me find every option and customization to meet specific course needs! This book represents the true application of the Gradebook in action.

I would also like to thank all at Packt Publishing, especially the reviewers, for their support while writing and updating this book.

About the Reviewers

David Le Blanc has BA, BEd, and MEd degrees. He is an experienced online guide, Moodle expert, and e-learning practitioner. He has been working on computer-based learning since the mid 1980s and in secondary education for the past 25 years. Currently, David works with local school districts and colleges to design online learning and support educators to deliver courses in the Moodle learning environment.

Belinda Caulfield has been working in Further education for 17 years, focusing on Information Learning Technologies (ILT) in teaching and learning for the last 10 years. She has worked as an ILT developer with the ILT development manager, Kevin Lawrence, on Moodle and Mahara environments, supporting staff and learners to use these technologies.

The newly merged college Coleg y Cymoedd is keen to see how Belinda uses ILT and mobile technologies in teaching and learning in her role as an ILT Developer. Belinda loves to encourage staff to use interactive whiteboards and enthusiastically supports them in their own development and the creation of interactive resources for them to use in their lessons.

She has also investigated new technologies such as Augmented Reality (AR) and mobile devices and how they can be used in teaching and learning.

She works full time at Coleg y Cymoedd and balances her life as a wife and mother with her love for learning technologies, social networking, and her hobby—crocheting portraits for her friends and family.

I would like to thank Rebecca Barrington for giving me the opportunity to review her book and Akash Poojary for supporting and introducing me to the new challenges of being a book reviewer.

Ann Morgan, M.Ed., Technology, was an educator for 27 years, teaching grades 2 to 8. For the last 4 years, she was an instructional technology specialist at Chatham, Massachusetts, where she began using Moodle in 2006, teaching grades 5 to 8. She currently spends her time exclusively as a Moodle course coach and consultant. Ann has earned the coveted Moodle Course Creator Certificate (MCCC) from `moodle.org`.

She is a member of the instructional and developmental teams for The Learning Curve Consortium. She teaches graduate credit online courses about Moodle and consults and coaches various institutions on Moodle implementation.

www.PacktPub.com

Support files, eBooks, discount offers, and more

For support files and downloads related to your book, please visit www.PacktPub.com.

Did you know that Packt offers eBook versions of every book published, with PDF and ePub files available? You can upgrade to the eBook version at www.PacktPub.com and as a print book customer, you are entitled to a discount on the eBook copy. Get in touch with us at service@packtpub.com for more details.

At www.PacktPub.com, you can also read a collection of free technical articles, sign up for a range of free newsletters and receive exclusive discounts and offers on Packt books and eBooks.

https://www2.packtpub.com/books/subscription/packtlib

Do you need instant solutions to your IT questions? PacktLib is Packt's online digital book library. Here, you can search, access, and read Packt's entire library of books.

Why subscribe?
- Fully searchable across every book published by Packt
- Copy and paste, print, and bookmark content
- On demand and accessible via a web browser

Free access for Packt account holders

If you have an account with Packt at www.PacktPub.com, you can use this to access PacktLib today and view 9 entirely free books. Simply use your login credentials for immediate access.

Table of Contents

Preface

Moodle is used in many areas of education to provide a range of resources and activities to support learning. However, it can also be used to manage learning and record progress.

This book will explain the uses of the Moodle grades area, also known as the Gradebook, where grades for completed work can be recorded and final grades can be calculated. You will also learn the different options for grading work, customizing how the grades appear, and how to view progress through a range of reports. This book is based on Moodle 2.7 and will highlight some of the core features within Moodle that complement the Gradebook.

The book will provide step-by-step instructions with screenshots to take you through setting up the Gradebook, adding tasks with grades, and reporting progress.

What this book covers

This book is an introduction to the Gradebook and explains how it can be used to manage assessments. It does not explain every option possible within the grades area and activities as there are too many. However, it will cover the most common elements that can be used and adapted to meet most course needs.

Chapter 1, *Introduction to Gradebook*, contains an overview of different elements of the Gradebook and how they apply to an online course. It sets the scene for the practical instructions provided throughout the book.

Chapter 2, *Customizing Grades*, contains step-by-step instructions on how to create your own custom scale (using statements rather than numbers) and use letter grades (letters or words linked to a percentage). Outcomes are also explained to enable more detailed recording within assessments.

Chapter 3, Adding Graded Activities, teaches you how to add assignments and customize them using the grading options available. Advanced grading methods are outlined to enable easy grading using multiple criteria.

Chapter 4, Assigning Grades, demonstrates the various ways in which assessments can be marked with written feedback and grades. The marking workflow and offline grading are also explained.

Chapter 5, Using Calculations, demonstrates the use of the Gradebook to calculate final grades for the online course. It covers the different options available during calculations and how each one can be used.

Chapter 6, Organizing the Gradebook Using Categories, shows you how to add categories to the Gradebook and move assignments into them. It also covers the ways to use categories to further customize how you use the Gradebook.

Chapter 7, Reporting with the Gradebook, shows you the different reports available to view all grades or individual user information, and explains how to export the Gradebook data.

Chapter 8, Additional Features for Progress Tracking, covers other features within Moodle that complement the Gradebook. We can use the activity and course completion features to provide an overview of student achievement.

How to use this book

Users who are new to Moodle assessments and the Gradebook can read this book from the beginning to the end and follow the instructions to get some practical experience. Users who are already familiar with the basics of the Gradebook can use each chapter individually to customize the Gradebook according to their needs.

If you would like to walk through the instructions in this book, you will need editing access to a course in Moodle 2.7.

You can also use the instructions if you are using an earlier version of Moodle. However, grading with rubrics is only available from Moodle 2.2 onwards, and the marking guide from 2.3. Similarly, the marking workflow is only featured from Moodle 2.6 and above. The Gradebook in Moodle 1.9 is also very similar to Moodle 2.x, so most of the instructions can still be followed if you are using earlier versions.

What you need for this book

This book assumes you already know the following topics:

- Accessing and navigating Moodle
- How to add resources and activities to Moodle

Some of the features and activities explained will need to be turned on within the site administration. Wherever this is required, it will be explained in an information box.

Who this book is for

Moodle Gradebook Second Edition is for anyone who uses Moodle as a course instructor or Moodle trainer. You will need to know the basic functions of using and navigating Moodle but no prior knowledge of the grades functions will be required.

Conventions

In this book, you will find a number of styles of text that distinguish between different kinds of information. Here are some examples of these styles and explanations of their meanings.

Code words in text, database table names, folder names, filenames, file extensions, pathnames, dummy URLs, user input, and Twitter handles are shown as follows: "For this example, we will call it `Core assignment criteria`."

New terms and **important words** are shown in bold. Words that you see on the screen, in menus or dialog boxes for example, appear in the text like this: "Click on **Save changes** at the bottom of the screen and go back to the main course screen".

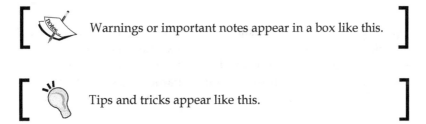

[Warnings or important notes appear in a box like this.]

[Tips and tricks appear like this.]

Reader feedback

Feedback from our readers is always welcome. Let us know what you think about this book—what you liked or may have disliked. Reader feedback is important for us to develop titles that you really get the most out of.

To send us general feedback, simply send an e-mail to feedback@packtpub.com, and mention the book title via the subject of your message.

If there is a topic that you have expertise in and you are interested in either writing or contributing to a book, see our author guide on www.packtpub.com/authors.

Customer support

Now that you are the proud owner of a Packt book, we have a number of things to help you to get the most from your purchase.

Errata

Although we have taken every care to ensure the accuracy of our content, mistakes do happen. If you find a mistake in one of our books—maybe a mistake in the text or the code—we would be grateful if you would report this to us. By doing so, you can save other readers from frustration and help us improve subsequent versions of this book. If you find any errata, please report them by visiting http://www.packtpub.com/submit-errata, selecting your book, clicking on the **errata submission form** link, and entering the details of your errata. Once your errata are verified, your submission will be accepted and the errata will be uploaded on our website, or added to any list of existing errata, under the Errata section of that title. Any existing errata can be viewed by selecting your title from http://www.packtpub.com/support.

Piracy

Piracy of copyright material on the Internet is an ongoing problem across all media. At Packt, we take the protection of our copyright and licenses very seriously. If you come across any illegal copies of our works, in any form, on the Internet, please provide us with the location address or website name immediately so that we can pursue a remedy.

Please contact us at copyright@packtpub.com with a link to the suspected pirated material.

We appreciate your help in protecting our authors, and our ability to bring you valuable content.

Questions

You can contact us at questions@packtpub.com if you are having a problem with any aspect of the book, and we will do our best to address it.

1
Introduction to Gradebook

If you are using **Moodle**, you are likely to deliver some form of course content or provide resources to others. You might do this to support learning, training, or for other educational activities. Many online courses, qualifications, or educational resources have a final goal, which is likely to include assessment or required elements to be completed. The Gradebook can be a valuable tool that will help the teacher manage the online course and track students' progress through assessment and required activities.

This chapter will introduce you to the Gradebook and the key features it offers. It will outline the benefits of using the Gradebook, the activities that can be graded and used within the Gradebook, and the types of grades that can be used. You will be given an overview of how it can be used to show progress before moving on to the rest of the chapters that will help you set up the different elements. In this chapter, you will learn:

- How to get to the Gradebook
- How the Gradebook is presented and how the information is provided
- Key features of the Gradebook
- Key activities that work with the Gradebook

Getting to the Gradebook

All courses in Moodle have a grades area, which is also known as the **Gradebook**. A number of activities within Moodle can be graded, and these grades will be automatically captured and shown in the Gradebook.

To get to the Gradebook, view the **Administration** block on the course and then click on **Grades** under the **Course administration** heading.

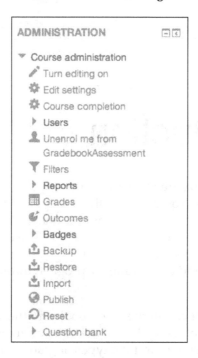

The following screenshot shows you an example of the teacher's view of a simple Gradebook with a number of different graded activities within it:

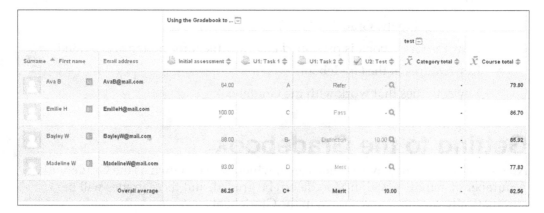

Let's take a quick tour of what we can see:

- The top row of the image shows you the column headings, which include each of the assessed activities within the Moodle course. Graded activities automatically appear in the grades area when they are added into the main course. In this case, the assessed activities are **Initial assessment, U1: Task 1, U1: Task 2**, and **U2: Test**.

- On the left-hand side of the image, you can see the students' names. Essentially, the name is the start of a row that includes all the information about a student. If we start with **Ava B** in the top row, we can see that she received a score of **64.00** for her initial assessment.

- Looking at **Bayley W**, we can see that he scored **10.00** for the **U2: Test**.

- Finally, we can see that **Madeline W** received **Merit** for **U1: Task 2**.

- On the far right-hand side of the table is **Course total**, which is calculated based on the grades entered for each assessed activity. By default, this shows you an average grade but the calculation can be changed when setting up the Gradebook. We will look at the different ways of calculating a course total in *Chapter 5, Using Calculations*.

- At the bottom of the table, you can see a row with **Overall average** in the first column. This row shows you the average of all the grades within each assessment type.

The Gradebook captures all the assessment information on one screen.

Users who have the roles of teacher, non-editing teacher, or manager will be able to see the grades for all students who are enrolled for the course. Students will only be able to see their own grades and feedback.

The advantage of storing the grades within Moodle is that information can be easily shared between all teachers in the online course. Traditionally, if a course manager wanted to know how students were progressing, they would need to contact the course teacher(s) to gather this information. Now, they can log in to Moodle and view the live data (as long as they have teacher or manager rights to the course).

There are benefits for students as well as they will see all their progress in one place and can start to manage their own learning by reviewing their progress to date, as shown in the following example of a student's view:

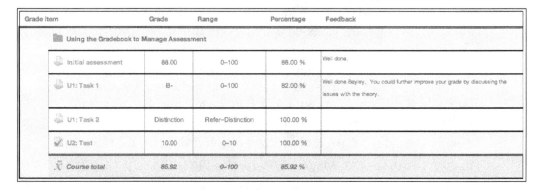

Grade Item	Grade	Range	Percentage	Feedback
Using the Gradebook to Manage Assessment				
Initial assessment	88.00	0–100	88.00 %	Well done.
U1: Task 1	B-	0–100	82.00 %	Well done Bayley. You could further improve your grade by discussing the issues with the theory.
U1: Task 2	Distinction	Refer–Distinction	100.00 %	
U2: Test	10.00	0–10	100.00 %	
Course total	85.92	0–100	85.92 %	

The grade report shown is of that of **Bayley W**. **Bayley** can see each assessment on the left-hand side with his grade next to it. By default, the student's grade report also shows the range of grades possible for the assessment (for example, the highest and lowest scores possible), but this can be switched off by the teacher in the Gradebook settings. This also shows you the equivalent percentage as well as any written feedback given by the teacher. The options for customizing reports will be explained further in *Chapter 7, Reporting with the Gradebook*.

Activities that work with the Gradebook

There are a number of Moodle activities that can be graded and, therefore, work with the Gradebook. The activities that will automatically appear in the Gradebook are:

- Assignments
- Quizzes
- Lessons
- The SCORM package
- Workshops

A number of other Moodle activities can also have grades and ratings assigned to them so that they also appear in the Gradebook. These include:

- Forums
- Glossaries

It is also possible to manually set up a *graded item* within the Gradebook, which is not linked with an activity but allows a grade to be recorded.

This book will not explain how to add all of these activities. However, *Chapter 3, Adding Graded Activities*, will provide an overview of the options within an assignment that is the most feature-rich of all of the graded Moodle items.

Key features of the Gradebook

The Gradebook primarily shows you the grade or score for each graded activity within the online course. This grade can be shown in a number of ways:

- **Numerical grade**: A numerical grade is already set up and ready for use within all Moodle courses with a default maximum score of 100 (a higher maximum can be set within site administration and this will be explained in *Chapter 2, Customizing Grades*).

- **Scale**: This refers to a customized grading profile that can be letters, words, statements, or numbers (such as Pass, Merit and Distinction).

- **Letter grade**: This refers to a grading profile that can be linked to percentages (such as one hundred percent = A).

Within some activities (such as assignments), written feedback can be provided in addition to the grade and can be viewed in the user reports and by students.

Organizing grades

With lots of activities that use grades within a course, the Gradebook will have a lot of data on one page. Categories can be created for group activities, and the Gradebook view can be customized according to the user for them to see all or some categories on the screen.

Think about a course that has 15 units and each unit has 3 assessments within it. The Gradebook will have 45 columns of grades, which is a lot of data! We can organize this information into categories in order to make it easier to use. We will be doing this in *Chapter 6, Organizing the Gradebook Using Categories*.

Summary

This chapter has given you a brief overview of the Gradebook, what it will show, how it can be used, and which activities feed into the grades area. It has only provided an introduction to the key features, but you can now work through each chapter and learn how to set them up in a way that works best for you.

As each element is explained in the following chapters, activities will be provided that will help you apply the ideas as well as provide a range of example uses. The default settings will be used for examples initially; however, where further customization is required, it will be explained within the chapters. These settings will mainly be changed at course level by a course teacher, and we will also highlight where these settings need to be switched on or amended by a site administrator.

In the next chapter, you will find out more about the different grading options and have a go at customizing scales and letter grades.

2
Customizing Grades

When creating a graded activity, you will choose how the activity will be scored and this score will automatically be added into the course's grades area.

The default grading options in a Moodle site are number grades (0–100) and a preset scale called **Separate and connected ways of knowing**.

 Scales are an option to grade assignments or rate forum posts with words rather than numbers. You can find out more about scales at https://docs.moodle.org/27/en/Separate_and_Connected_ways_of_knowing.

Different courses will use different grading conventions, and the ability to customize grades to meet specific course requirements is sometimes required. Letter grades can be customized and scales can be created by teachers within a course and site-wide scales, known as **Standard scales**, can be created by a Moodle administrator.

In this chapter, the different grading options will be outlined and you will be given some uses of each grade type. You will create your own custom scales using words or statements, customize the letter grades, and set up outcomes. The considerations for calculating final grades and adding grades together will also be outlined in relation to each grade type.

Numeric grades

100 is the default grade for all assessments in Moodle. When setting up a graded activity, you will choose the highest grade possible for that assignment (such as 50), and when marking the assignment, you will assign the grade achieved. No other changes need to be made in order to use numerical grades from 0–100. However, if you want to grade assignments with scores higher than 100, an administrator can change the maximum grade possible within **Site administration** area.

Site administrators can change the highest numerical grade possible by navigating to **Site Administration | Grades | General settings**. Find the **Grade point maximum** section and add the maximum number for assignments across the site.

Numeric grades are the simplest type of grading used to calculate course scores. Numbers are always easier to add than words!

Letter grades

For some assessments or homework activities, students might need to see their assignment graded with a letter such **A** or **D**. In Moodle, **letter grades** are essentially number grades that are shown as letters in the Gradebook. Percentages are used to link the grade awarded to a relevant letter grade. The advantage of using letter grades is that they act like numbers, so they can be used for a course's total calculations.

The default grade letters within Moodle courses are shown in the following screenshot:

Edit grade letters

Highest	Lowest	Letter
100.00 %	93.00 %	A
92.99 %	90.00 %	A-
89.99 %	87.00 %	B+
86.99 %	83.00 %	B
82.99 %	80.00 %	B-
79.99 %	77.00 %	C+
76.99 %	73.00 %	C
72.99 %	70.00 %	C-
69.99 %	67.00 %	D+
66.99 %	60.00 %	D
59.99 %	0.00 %	F

Edit grade letters

When the teacher grades the assignment, they give a numerical grade, which is then converted by Moodle into a percentage and is shown as the relevant grade letter in the Gradebook.

For example, if the course uses the default letter grades and an assignment is given a grade of **85**%, the letter grade shown in the Gradebook will be **B** because the grade is between **83.00**% and **86.99**%, as shown in the preceding screenshot.

The letter grades can be customized to link to any percentage in order to meet the course's needs. The letters can also be changed into words.

Customizing letter grades

The ability to edit the grade letters to meet specific course needs enables us to present information in the Gradebook to staff and students, which has more meaning than numbers alone can provide. For example, if our student needs to achieve 60 percent to pass the assignment, we can customize the letter grades to indicate that anything graded at 60 percent or more shows the word **Pass** as the grade, and anything below 60 percent shows the word **Fail**. This will make more sense to the student than the number grade. Let's set up an example and see an alternative use of the letter grades.

Creating a letter grade that uses words

In this example, we are going to set up letter grades that enable teachers to grade the assignment out of 36, which will be the grade that will be required in order to gain a distinction for each assessment. However, if the student does not meet all the criteria, they can gain a lower grade (either a pass or a merit). If they don't meet enough criteria, the assignment will be graded as **Not yet complete**. The teacher will score the assignment with the numbers, but the students will see the word as their grade. When we come to set up the final course total, Moodle will make use of the numbers in order to calculate the final grade.

In order to ensure the letter grades show **pass**, **merit**, or **distinction**, we need to customize the letter grades to show these words and identify the equivalent percentage for the differing grade levels. The following table shows you the final grade linked to the different grade levels and the calculated percentage:

Grade	Minimum grade	Percentage
Distinction	36	100 percent (36/36*100)
Merit	27	75 percent (27/36*100)
Pass	18	50 percent (18/36*100)
Not yet complete	Below 18	49.9 percent or lower

The percentage is calculated through this formula: Minimum grade divided by maximum grade (in this case 36) and multiplied by 100.

The percentages used in letter grades are set to two decimal places and require a maximum and minimum percentage per letter grade. The full range needs to extend from **0.00%** to **100.00%**.

So, let's set this up in a Moodle course using the following steps:

1. Within the course, navigate to **Administration | Course administration | Grades**.

2. Once you are in the **Grades** area, you will either see a drop-down list, tabs, or both (the view you will see will depend on the settings made by your site administrator). If you're using the **Grader report** drop-down list, navigate to **Letters | View**. If you're using **Tabs**, click on **Letters**. You can also access the letter grades area by clicking on **Letters** in the **Administration** block.

 The default setting is the drop-down menu, but this can be changed by navigating to **Site administration | Grades | General settings** and changing the **Navigation method**.

3. Click on **Edit grade letters**.

4. Click on **Override site defaults** so that a tick appears in the box.

   We need to set the grade letter and grade boundary for each item that we would like to use in the course. Use the table that shows you the percentages for pass, merit, and distinction (shown previously) to set up the grade letters, as shown in the following screenshot. Letter grade boundary is the minimum score required to get a particular grade. Start from the top (100%) and work down the list. Once you have added 0%, all the other letter grades need to be set as unused. You do not need to worry about removing any grade letters shown in the Grade letter field. They will simply be ignored once the Letter grade boundary drop-down list has been set to unused.

5. Click on **Save changes** at the bottom of the screen and you will see a table similar to the one shown in the following screenshot. If you need to change these grades at any time, you can click on **Edit grade letters**, or if you are on the main course screen, you can navigate to **Administration | Grades | Letters | Edit**.

These letter grades are now set up for use in the course.

	Edit grade letters	
Highest	**Lowest**	**Letter**
100.00 %	100.00 %	Distinction
99.99 %	75.00 %	Merit
74.99 %	50.00 %	Pass
49.99 %	0.00 %	Not yet complete

Note that by adding the grade boundaries (in this case, the minimum score required to gain each grade), Moodle will calculate the maximum percentage in order to ensure that the grade profile ranges from **0.00%** to **100.00%**.

When we come to set up a graded activity that shows the letters, we will also need to make some changes within the Gradebook; we will see how to do this in *Chapter 5, Using Calculations*.

Only one set of letter grades can be used per course. Therefore, whenever letter grades are used, they will always use the letters set up for that course. So, in the course that we are using in this example, now that we have set up the pass, merit, and distinction letter grades, the original default **A** to **D** plus **F** grading (shown in the first image in this chapter) will no longer be available within this course. You can, however, have multiple scales within your course.

Creating scales to grade assignments

Scales are a list of words or characters that can be used to grade assignments. Each scale needs at least two choices, but you can have as many words in the scale as you want. You can also use lots of different scales within one course. Examples of scales include the following:

- Refer or pass
- Unsatisfactory, satisfactory, good, or outstanding
- Reviewed or feedback given
- Fail, pass, merit, or distinction

The scale is created prior to the graded activity being added to the course, and when an activity is added to the course, the required scale can be selected. When marking an assignment, the teacher is given the scale options in a drop-down list so that they can select the grade to be awarded. It should be noted that after a scale has been used, it can no longer be edited.

Scales are useful when assignments are assessed using words or phrases or when a course needs to use a range of different grades in order to provide feedback to learners (as we are only able to have one set of letter grades per course). Scales can be used in a range of contexts, including the use of academic terminology as a grade (such as Pass or Complete) or the use of descriptive text to give useful feedback (such as work reviewed or please speak to your teacher).

Scales can still be used to calculate final grades, but the scores are based on the number of items in the scale rather than a specific score for each element of the scale. Think about a scale that contains two options: Not yet complete and complete. In this example, the scale will be based on a maximum score of 2 (one point for Not yet complete and two points for Complete). However, additional weightings can be used to increase the point value. The use of weightings will be explained in *Chapter 5, Using Calculations*.

Calculating scores using scales can be confusing and therefore, scales are not always the best option when complex scoring is required. However, for courses that use simple calculations or where there is a point at which a learner will pass, scales can be a useful way to present course grades that will make sense to students.

Customizing grade scales

In the example used earlier, we used **Not yet complete**, **pass**, **merit**, and **distinction** as grade letters, but this could also easily be added as a word scale. We will set this one up as a scale to see how the scoring will be different:

1. Within the course, navigate to **Administration** | **Site administration** | **Grades**.

2. Once you're in the **Grades** area, you will either see a drop-down list or tabs (or both). If you're using the drop-down list, navigate to **Scales** | **View**. If you're using the tabs, click on **Scales**.

3. At the bottom of this screen, click on **Add a new scale**.

4. In the **Name** box, give the **Scale** option a title. In this case, give it the name PMD in order to identify it as **pass**, **merit**, and **distinction**. This name is used when you choose to use the scale, so it needs to be easy to identify and differentiate it from any other available scales.

 If you would like to use a scale that is available site-wide, an administrator also has the option to set this as a standard scale by checking the box. Teachers will not be able to choose this option.

In the **Scale** box, we will write each word that we would like to appear in the grading list, each one separated by a comma. It needs to start with the negative scale item first and end with a positive scale item (that is, the first scale item should be the lowest grade with each scale item increasing and the final scale item as the highest grade). For this example, complete the **Scale** box, as shown in the following screenshot:

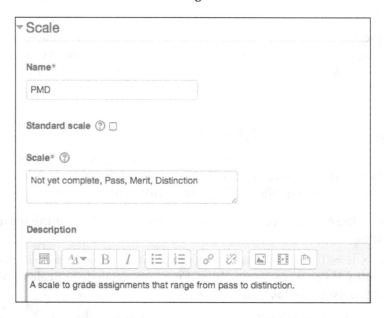

5. In the **Description** box, provide a brief explanation of the scale and/or its use. This is particularly important for standard (site-wide) scales, as teachers might choose to use it even though they haven't created it themselves.

6. Click on **Save changes** to save this scale. It is now available for use.

We will look at how this will be scored when we look at category aggregation in *Chapter 5, Using Calculations*. However, it will use one of the two grading profiles:

Not yet complete	Pass	Merit	Distinction
0	1	2	3
1	2	3	4

You can see how this will be calculated in a way that is different from the letter grade percentages used earlier.

Have another go!

Let's also set up a simple scale that we can use later so that we can practice how to add these custom scales.

Create a scale called `Completion` with three options: `Not yet complete`, `Partially complete`, and `Complete`. Remember to add them in negative to positive order.

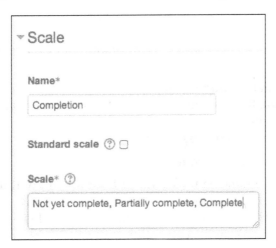

Using Outcomes

Outcomes are extra elements that can be added to a graded activity in order to be able to grade specific elements that have been completed. Each outcome can be graded with **Scale**, but the teacher must also put in an overall grade for the graded activity. Outcomes can be especially useful for courses that require students to demonstrate competency against specific performance criteria. When we add a graded activity, we will choose which outcomes, if any, it links with (you do not have to use all outcomes on all assessments).

We will set up some outcomes to enable us to assess whether specific criteria is completed and evidence has been provided. We will make use of the `Completion` scale that we have just set up.

In order for outcomes to be set up in a course, they need to be enabled site-wide by an administrator. The setting can be turned on by navigating to **Site administration | Advanced features** and adding a tick next to **Enable outcomes**. Click on **Save changes** at the bottom of the screen. Once this has been done, an **Outcomes** option will appear in the course settings block.

We will create three outcomes that we can use to assess elements of the assignment. These will be as follows:

- Criteria 1 met
- Criteria 2 met
- Evidence provided

Let's add the outcomes according to the following steps:

1. Within the course, navigate to **Administration** | **Course administration** | **Grades**.

2. Once you're in the **Grades** area, you will either see a drop-down list or tabs, as before. If using the drop-down list, navigate to **Outcomes** | **Edit outcomes**. If you're using the tabs, click on **Outcomes** and then click on **Edit outcomes**, which appears under the tabs menu.

3. Click on **Add a new outcome**.

4. We will use the same name for the **Full name** and **Short name** boxes in order to prevent confusion later (the short name is only used in the outcome report, but it is best to keep the full name short as this will get displayed in the Gradebook). We will keep both names short.

5. We need to add the outcomes in the reverse order in order to ensure that they appear in the correct order in the Gradebook. In the **Full name** and **Short name** box, type in Evidence provided.

6. In the **Scale** drop-down box, choose the **Completion** scale we created earlier.

7. In the **Description** box, you can add more details for the outcome in case others use it (in this case, write `All evidence required has been submitted or seen by the teacher`).

8. Click on **Save changes** at the bottom of the screen.

Repeat this process for the following two outcomes:

Full name and short name	Scale	Description
Criteria 2 met	Completion	All elements of criteria 2 have been met
Criteria 1 met	Completion	All elements of criteria 1 have been met

When you have saved changes for the final time, your **Custom outcomes** screen should look like the following screenshot:

Custom outcomes

Full name	Short name	Scale	Items	Edit
Evidence provided	Evidence provided	Completion	0	⚙ ✕
Criteria 2 met	Criteria 2 met	Completion	0	⚙ ✕
Criteria 1 met	Criteria 1 met	Completion	0	⚙ ✕

It is worth noting that outcomes can only be deleted before they are added to an assignment. Once it is used in an assignment, the delete option will not be available, but you will still be able to edit. However, if the outcome is removed from all assignments, we will be able to delete the outcome from the course. We will look at how these outcomes are added to an assignment in *Chapter 3, Adding Graded Activities*.

Summary

Through the use of numerical grades, letter grades, and scales, a teacher can customize their Gradebook to ensure that it can meet the specific course requirements. Where required, a teacher can also make use of outcomes that can be used in conjunction with a scale to demonstrate competency against specific criteria. Each type of grade has its own benefits, but the options you would like to calculate the final grade should be considered before you choose your grade type in order to ensure that it meets your needs. Remember that numerical grades or grade letters can always be calculated in a more straightforward manner than word grades (scales). Scales should only be used when no grading or only simple grading is required. However, numerical grades and letter grades can be used for more complex grading requirements.

We will now take a look at how to add these grading options to assignments within Moodle before you learn how to grade work.

3
Adding Graded Activities

In this chapter, we will look at how to add assignments and set up how they will be graded, including how to use our custom scales and add outcomes for grading. We will also see how to add additional graded items to the Gradebook.

As with all content within Moodle, we need to select **Turn editing on** within the course in order to be able to add resources and activities. All graded activities are added through the **Add an activity or resource text** available within each section of within a Moodle course. This text can be found in the bottom right of each section after editing has been turned on. As outlined in *Chapter 1, Introduction to Gradebook*, there are a number of items that can be graded and will appear within the Gradebook. Assignments are the most feature-rich of all the graded activities and have many options available in order to customize how assessments can be graded. They can be used to provide assessment information for students, store grades, and provide feedback. When setting up the assignment, we can choose for students to submit their work electronically—either through file submission or online text, or we can review the assessment offline and use only the grade and feedback features of the assignment.

Adding assignments

There are many options within the assignments, and throughout this chapter we will set up a number of different assignments and you'll learn about some of their most useful features and options. Let's have a go at creating a range of assignments that are ready for grading in *Chapter 4, Assigning Grades*.

Creating an assignment with a scale

The first assignment that we will add will make use of the **PMD** scale that we created in *Chapter 2, Customizing Grades*:

1. Click on the **Turn editing** on button.

2. Click on **Add an activity or resource**.

3. Click on **Assignment** and then click on **Add**.

4. In the **Assignment name** box, type in the name of the assignment (such as Task 1).

5. In the **Description** box, provide some assignment details.

6. In the **Availability** section, we need to disable the date options. We will not make use of these options, but they can be very useful. To disable the options, click on the tick next to the **Enable** text.

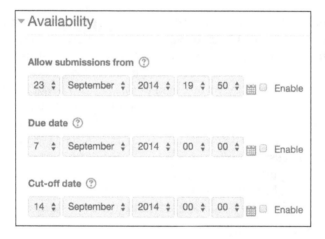

However, details of these options have been provided for future reference.

- The **Allow submissions from** section is mostly relevant when the assignment will be submitted electronically, as students won't be able to submit their work until the date and time indicated here.

- The **Due date** section can be used to indicate when the assignment needs to be submitted by. If students electronically submit their assignment after the date and time indicated here, the submission date and time will be shown in red in order to notify the teacher that it was submitted past the due date.

- The **Cut off date** section enables teachers to set an extension period after the due date where late submissions will continue to be accepted.

7. In the **Submission types** section, ensure that the **File submissions** checkbox is enabled by adding a tick there. This will enable students to submit their assignment electronically. There are additional options that we can choose as well. With **Maximum number of uploaded files**, we can indicate how many files a student can upload. Keep this as **1**. We can also determine the **Maximum submission size** option for each file using the drop-down list shown in the following screenshot:

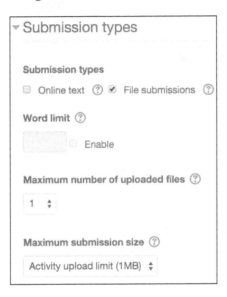

8. Within the **Feedback types** section, ensure that all options under the **Feedback types** section are selected.

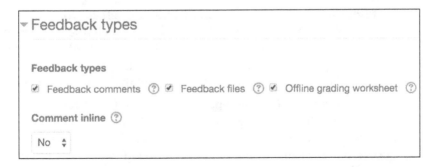

   ○ **Feedback comments** enables us to provide written feedback along with the grade.

   ○ **Feedback files** enables us to upload a file in order to provide feedback to a student.

- Offline grading worksheet will provide us with the option to download a .csv file that contains core information about the assignment, and this can be used to add grades and feedback while working offline. This completed .csv file can be uploaded and the grades will be added to the assignments within the Gradebook.

9. In the **Submission settings** section, we have options related to how students will submit their assignment and how they will reattempt submission if required.

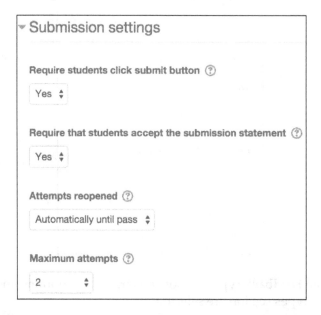

- If **Require students click submit button** is left as **No**, students will upload their assignment and it will be available to the teacher for grading. If this option is changed to **Yes**, students can upload their assignment, but the teacher will see that it is in the draft form. Students will click on **Submit** to indicate that it is ready to be graded.

- **Require that students accept the submission statement** will provide students with a statement that they need to agree to when they submit their assignment. The default statement is **This assignment is my own work, except where I have acknowledged the use of works of other people**.

 The submission statement can be changed by a site administrator by navigating to **Site administration | plugins | Activity modules | Assignment settings**.

- ○ The **Attempts reopened** drop-down list provides options for the status of the assignment after it has been graded. Students will only be able to resubmit their work when it is open. Therefore this setting will control when and if students are able to submit another version of their assignment. The options available to us are:

  Never: This option should be selected if students will not be able to submit another piece of work.

  Manually: This will enable anyone who has the role of a teacher to choose to reopen a submission that enables a student to submit their work again.

  Automatically until pass: This option works when a pass grade is set within the Gradebook. This will be explained in *Chapter 8, Additional Features for Progress Tracking*. After grading, if the student is awarded the minimum pass grade or higher, the submission will remain closed in order to prevent any changes to the submission. However, if the assignment is graded lower than the assigned pass grade, the submission will automatically reopen in order to enable the student to submit the assignment again.

  Maximum attempts: The maximum attempts allowed for this assignment will limit the number of times an assignment is reopened. For example, if this option is set to **3**, then a student will only be able to submit their assignment three times. After they have submitted their assignment for a third time, they will not be allowed to submit it again. The default is **unlimited**, but it can be changed by clicking on the drop-down list.

10. In the **Submission settings** section, ensure that the options for **Require students click on submit button** and **Require that students accept the submission statement** are set to **Yes**. Also, change the **Attempts reopened** to **Automatically until passed**.

11. Within the **Grade** section, navigate to **Grade | Type | Scale** and choose the **PMD** scale created within *Chapter 2, Customizing Grades*. Select **Use marking workflow** by changing the drop-down list to **Yes**.

    Use marking workflow is a new feature of **Moodle 2.6** that enables the grading process to go through a range of stages in order to indicate that the marking is in progress or is complete, is being reviewed, or is ready for release to students. This will be explained in more detail in *Chapter 4, Assigning Grades*.

12. Click on **Save and return to course**.

Creating an online assignment with a number grade

The next assignment that we will create will have an online text option that will have a maximum grade of 20. The following steps show you how to create an online assignment with a number grade:

1. Enable editing by clicking on **Turn editing on**.

2. Click on **Add an activity or resource**.

3. Click on **Assignment** and then click on **Add**.

4. In the **Assignment name** box, type in the name of the assignment (such as Task 2).

5. In the **Description** box, provide the assignment details.

6. In the **Submission types** section, ensure that **Online text** has a tick next to it. This will enable students to type directly into Moodle. When choosing this option, we can also set a maximum word limit by clicking on the tick box next to the **Enable** text. After enabling this option, we can add a number to the textbox. For this assignment, enable a word limit of 200 words.

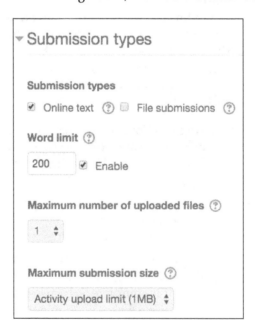

7. When using online text submission, we have an additional feedback option within the **Feedback types** section. Under the **Comment inline** text, click on **No** and switch to **Yes** to enable yourself to add written feedback for students within the written text submitted by students.

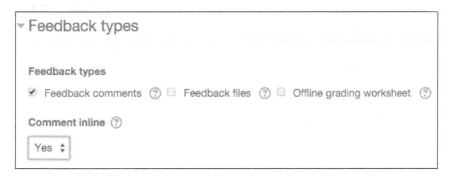

8. In the **Submission settings** section, ensure that the options for **Require students click submit button** and **Require that students accept the submission statement** are set to **Yes**. Also, change **Attempts reopened** to **Automatically until passed**.

9. Within the **Grades** section, navigate to **Grade | Type | Point** and ensure that **Maximum points** is set to 20.

10. Click on **Save and return to course**.

Creating an assignment including outcomes

The next assignment that we will create will add some of the Outcomes created in *Chapter 2, Customizing Grades*:

1. Enable editing by clicking on **Turn editing on.**

2. Click on **Add an activity or resource**.

3. Click on **Assignment** and then click on **Add**.

4. In the **Assignment name** box, type in the name of the assignment (such as Task 3).

5. In the **Description** box, provide the assignment details.

6. In the **Submission types** box, ensure that **Online text** and **File submissions** are selected. Set **Maximum number of uploaded files** to **2**.

7. In the **Submission settings** section, ensure that the options for **Require students to click submit button** and **Require that students accept the submission statement** are amended to **Yes**. Change **Attempts reopened** to **Manually**.

8. Within the **Grades** section, navigate to **Grade | Type | Point** and **Maximum points** is set to `100`.

9. In the **Outcomes** section, choose the outcomes as **Evidence provided** and **Criteria 1 met**.

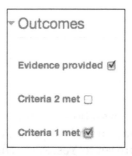

10. Scroll to the bottom of the screen and click on **Save and return to course**.

Alternative grading methods

Within the **Grade** section, there are three types of grading methods, and so far, we have only used the default **Simple direct grading** option. However, there are two other types of grading methods: **Marking guide** and **Rubric**.

The simple direct grading option enables us to choose the grade options (such as number or a scale), and the teacher adds the grade that is awarded to the student. The alternative grading methods use a very different grading process. The teacher does not select the final overall grade but grades individual criteria instead, and the score for each of these is added together to create the final grade. When creating an assignment that uses **Marking guide** or **Rubric**, we need to identify the criteria that will be used to assess the assignment.

The marking guide method

The marking guide's grading method allows us to add criteria and identify a top grade for each piece of criteria. When grading the assignment, the teacher will choose the grade to be awarded and can also add specific feedback. We will be setting up three criteria, two with a top mark of 5 and one with a top mark of 10.

If the student is graded with the top marks for each of the three criteria, they will receive the maximum grade of twenty. Let's add this together:

1. Click on the **Turn editing on** button.

2. Click on **Add an activity or resource**.

3. Click on **Assignment** and then click on **Add**.

4. In the **Assignment name** box, type in the name of the assignment (such as Assignment 4).

5. In the **Description box**, provide the assignment details.

6. Within the **Grades** section, navigate to **Grade | Type** and set it to **Point** and ensure that **Maximum points** is set to 20. Change **Grading method** to **Marking guide** using the drop-down list.

> Please note that the criteria does not need to add up to the maximum grade given for the assignment, as Moodle will convert the final grade received for the assignment to a decimal (by adding together the grade awarded for each criterion and dividing this by 100). This will be multiplied by the maximum grade set for the assignment. This is a normalization process that is explained in much more detail in *Chapter 5, Using Calculations*.

7. Scroll to the bottom of the screen and click on **Save and display**.

The next step is to set up the marking guide, where the screen will look like the following screenshot:

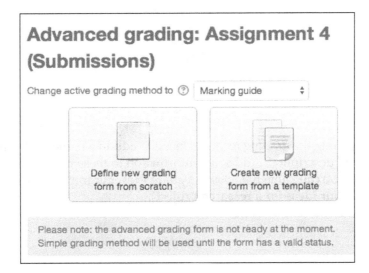

The previous screenshot lets us know that the advanced grading form is not yet ready and we have a choice between **Define a new grading form from scratch** and **Create new grading from a template**. If no marking guide is created at this stage, the assignment will make use of the standard direct grading method when the assignment is assessed.

8. Select **Define new grading form from scratch**.

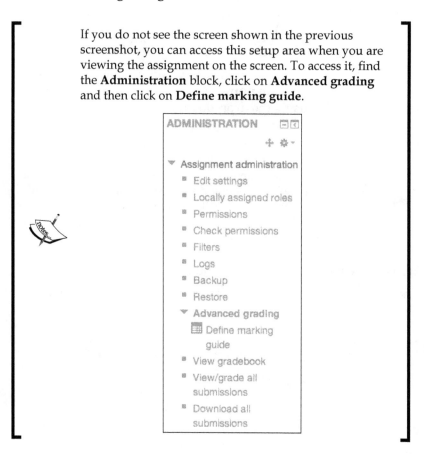

If you do not see the screen shown in the previous screenshot, you can access this setup area when you are viewing the assignment on the screen. To access it, find the **Administration** block, click on **Advanced grading** and then click on **Define marking guide**.

9. After opening the grading form, we need to add in a name for the marking guide and description. Add some information to these boxes (for the following example, we can name the marking guide **Presentation** and the description **Present your ideas for a research project**).

10. The next section is the actual **Marking guide** setup area, which has a place to add the first criterion. There are three elements for each criterion:

    ○ **Description for Students**: This is the information that a student will see in order to find out the assignment criteria. This will only be shown if the option for students to view the criteria is turned on.

    ○ **Description for Markers**: This information will be seen by teachers when they are grading the work and will help the teacher identify the grade to be awarded to the student.

    ○ **Maximum mark**: A teacher can choose the maximum grade possible for this criteria. When grading, the teacher can choose any grade from zero to this maximum number.

Marking guide

Click to edit criterion name
Description for Students

Description for Markers
Click to edit
Maximum mark
Click to edit

+ Add criterion

11. Under the **Marking guide** title, click on the **Click to edit** criterion name and add the text `Planning`.

12. Under the **Description for Students** title, click on **Click to edit**. Add the this to the box: `The presentation has been planned to include an initial overview plus as outline of each type of research.`

13. Within the **Description for Markers** section, click on the **Click to edit** text and add: `To gain top marks the overview must be very clear including the research question. There needs to be at least three types of research. There are five marks possible and should be based on 1 point for each item (clear overview, research question, three types of research).`

14. Finally, click on **Click to edit** under the **Maximum mark** title and add in the number 5. We now need to add some more criteria. Click on the **Add criterion** button and repeat the preceding process for the following criteria:

Criterion name	Description for students	Description for markers	Maximum mark
Presentation	The presentation is clearly and confidently presented	The student presented confidently with evidence that he/she planned and practiced the presentation. The student presented without reading a script. The presentation aids were appropriate, clear, and had the information required for the project.	10
Questions	The questions are answered at end of the presentation	The maximum points should be awarded if students were able to answer questions confidently, displaying understanding of their project. Lower points will be awarded if students were required to use their notes to answer questions or if they were unable to answer questions.	5

15. The next section to set up a marking guide is the **Frequently used comments** area where we can add statements that can be used when grading the assignment. Click on **Add frequently used comment** and type in Confidently presented and Evidence of planning and preparation.

16. Finally, we have two marking guide options that can be turned on and off using the tick boxes. Keep both of these turned on.

Your completed marking guide should look like this:

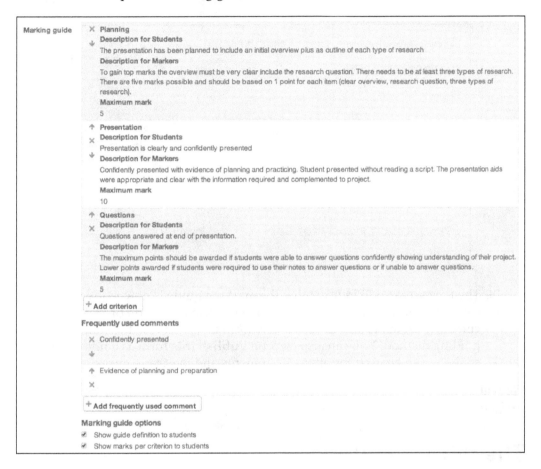

17. Click on **Save marking guide and make it ready**.

If we have not completed our marking guide, we can click on **Save as draft** and then come back to it via the **Advanced grading** link within the assignment administration block.

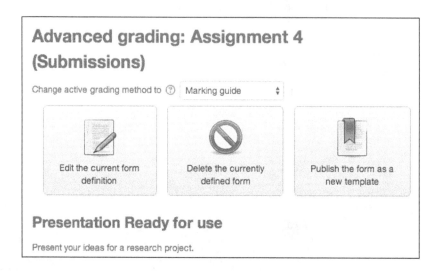

18. The next screen will indicate that the marking guide is now ready for use. You can still click on **Edit the Current form definition** or **Delete the currently defined form** to start a new form or to revert to the simple direct grading method. You can also click on **Publish this form as a new template** so that it can be used for other assignments and in other courses.

We will look at how to grade work using the marking guide in *Chapter 4, Assigning Grades*.

The rubrics method

The second method of alternative grading is called Rubrics. **Rubrics** allow a set of criteria to be set up for the assessment along with descriptors that outline the different levels at which the criteria are met. Each descriptor has a value that enables Moodle to calculate a final grade for the assessment based on the criteria met. Rubrics are a more detailed version of the marking guide, and they make the grading process simple for the teacher and students.

When using the Rubric grading method, we will need to create a grading form in a similar way in order to create the marking guide. We will set up a rubric assignment together:

1. Click on **Turn editing on** button.

2. Click on **Add an activity or resource**.

3. Click on **Assignment** and then click on **Add**.

4. In the **Assignment name** box, type in the name of the assignment (such as `Assignment 5`).

5. In the **Description** box, provide the assignment details as `Core criteria of an assignment`.

6. Within the **Grades** section navigate to **Grade | Type** and set it to **Point** and ensure that **Maximum points** is set to `30`. Change **Grading method** to **Rubric**.

7. Scroll to the bottom of the screen and click on **Save and display**. You will see an advanced grading screen like the one shown in the following screenshot:

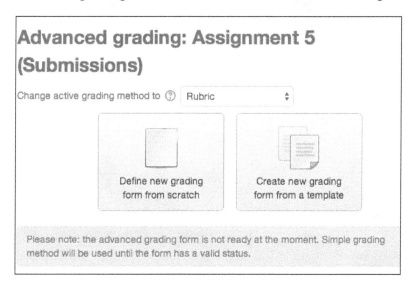

8. From this screen, we will choose the **Define new grading form from scratch** option. However, note that you can also select **Create new grading form from a template**. This enables you to use grading forms that you have already created in this or other courses or use standard (site-wide) forms created on the Moodle site.

As with the marking guide, if no rubric form is created at this stage, the simple direct grading method will be used; this means that the teacher will manually add in the final grade rather than grade the assignment using the criteria.

9. As this is the first form we have created, click on **Define new grading form from scratch**. The following screenshot will appear:

10. In the **Name** box, type in the name for this set of rubric criteria. For this example, we will call it Core assignment criteria. You can also add a description to the **Description** box (this is useful when sharing rubrics or searching for your own rubrics in order to use them as templates).

We will be completing the rubric criterion and level boxes, but first let's find out how rubrics are used and what these options are.

Within a rubric, there is at least one criterion, and each criterion has specific levels of grading. The criterion is an element of the assignment that needs to be met. The levels are the extent to which this criterion has been met. Statements are added and are used to assess the work, and when grading we can choose the relevant statement based on the extent to which this criterion has been met. For assignments that have multiple criteria, the points awarded for each criterion are added together to create the final grade.

The default setting within a rubric is for one criterion, with three points levels ranging from zero to two points. Additional criterion as well as additional grading levels for each criterion can be added (the number of grading levels can also be removed so that there can be fewer than three grading levels). The points awarded for each level can also be amended.

We will be setting up three criteria, each with a top grade of 10. If the student is graded the top marks for each of the three criteria, they will receive the top grade of 30 (we set 30 as the maximum grade when we added the assignment).

 As with the marking guide, the criteria does not need to always add up to the maximum grade given for the assignment, as a normalization process will convert the grade. This will be explained in *Chapter 5, Using Calculations*.

You can see the criteria we will be using in the following table; we will be using the same point system for each level in this example:

Criterion	0 points	3 points	6 points	10 points
The assignment should be 1,000 words	The word count is below 800 words or over 1,200 words	The word count is between 800 and 1,049 words	The word count is between 1,050 and 1,200 words	The assignment is between 1,000 and 1,050 words
At least 5 quotes should be used and be correctly referenced	No quotes used or quotes used but not referenced	Some quotes included but not fully referenced	5 quotes included and partly referenced	5 or more quotes included and correctly referenced
The assignment brief met (4 elements)	2 or fewer elements covered	3 elements covered	4 elements covered but more detail could be included	All 4 elements covered in detail

Let's add these criteria and levels to the course. We will add the first one together:

1. Click on the gray **Click to edit criterion** text to add the criteria detail.

2. Type in the first criterion (`The assignment should be 1000 words`). You can make the text box larger by holding your cursor in the bottom-right section of the box and dragging the box to make it bigger.

3. Click on the gray **Click to edit level** text in the box on the right-hand side of the criterion we have just added. This is where we need to type the statement for the zero points level shown in the preceding table (`The word count is below 800 words or over 1200 words`). Make sure the **points** box reads `0`.

4. Click on the next gray **Click to edit level** text in the box (currently, the `1` points level). Type in the three points level statement from the table. Change the points number to `3`.

5. Click on the last available level box and add in the six points statement and change the number of points to `6`.

6. We have now run out of the default number of levels but we still need to add the ten points level. Click on the **Add level** button on the right-hand side of the current level that we are working on.

7. Add in the level statement for ten points and change the points to `10`.

8. Click anywhere on the screen to finalize this text.

9. We now need to add another line for the next criterion. Under the current criterion, there is a **Add criterion** button. Click on this and an additional row to add another criterion and the level statements and points will appear. Use the preceding table to complete this rubric. Once completed, your rubric table should look like this:

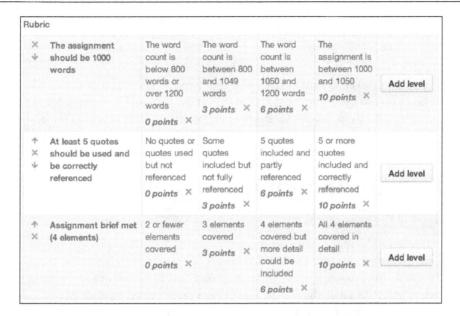

10. Underneath the criteria section of the rubric creation page, there are a number of options that show you how the rubric can be used. The text explains the options, and these are turned on by adding a tick and turned off by removing the tick. Keep them all turned on, as shown in the following screenshot:

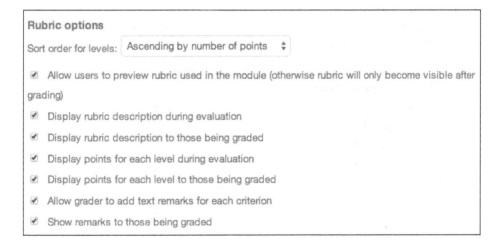

11. Scroll to the bottom of the screen and click on **Save rubric and make it ready**.

12. The rubric is now ready for use when grading the assignment. We will look at how to grade this in the next chapter.

13. If you want to edit your rubric, you will need to use the **Administration** block when you are viewing the assignment on the screen. Click on **Advanced grading** and then choose **Define rubric**, which will take you to the Rubric editing screen.

Adding additional grading directly into the Gradebook

We have looked at how we can add graded activities to a Moodle course so that they can be awarded a mark and used with the Gradebook. This is the main way in which we grade an assessment, as the students need to complete something in order to be graded (such as an assignment, quiz, discussion, or any other Moodle activity). We can also use the assignment tool to provide feedback on a student's assignment even if the students do not submit any work online, such as class presentations or practical work.

However, what if we would like a grade that is not linked to an activity to be added to the Gradebook? Perhaps students receive an additional grade based on their attendance in lessons. You might want the grade to be in the Gradebook for the final course grade but you do not want it to appear as an activity within the Moodle course. This is where a **Graded item**, added directly into the Moodle Gradebook, can be useful. The following steps indicate the steps to be followed:

1. From the main course screen, find the **Administration** block and click on **Grades** to get to the Gradebook.

2. Go into the **Categories and items** screen (click on the **Categories and items** tab on the top of the page if the tabs are available. Otherwise, click on the drop-down list and click on **Simple view** under the **categories and items** heading).

3. Scroll to the bottom of the screen and click on the **Add** grade item. The following screenshot will appear:

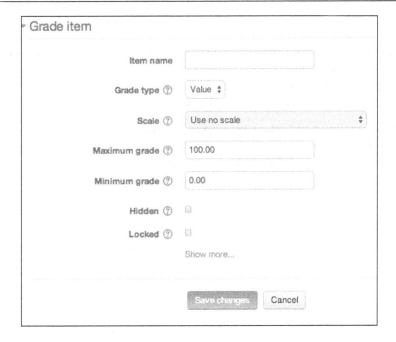

4. Give the graded item a name (add in the `Attendance grade` title).

    There are four **Grade types** available for graded items:

    ○ **Value**: This enables a number grade to be awarded. If this is used, the maximum and minimum grades possible can be set. For this example, we will keep the default options of **Minimum grade** `0.00` and **Maximum grade** `100.00`).

    ○ **Scale**: This allows you to choose a scale that is available within the course in order to grade this item. If this is chosen, the scale's drop-down list becomes available to enable us to choose the scale we would like to use.

    ○ **Text**: This does not allow any grade to be used, but written feedback can be added. This will not be used in Gradebook calculations.

    ○ **None**: This means that no grade is assigned to this item.

5. Click on **Save changes** at the bottom of the screen and go back to the main course screen.

Summary

In this chapter, we added a range of assignments that made use of number and scale grades as well as added outcomes to an assignment. We also added two assignments using the advanced grading methods that will enable us to grade assignments using specific criteria. Finally, we added a graded item directly into the Gradebook.

In the next chapter, we will look at grading assessments. We will add number and scale grades, add written feedback, grade outcomes, and make use of the marking guides and rubrics we created. We will also review the options within the marking workflow, use the offline grading worksheet, and grade work directly within the Gradebook.

4
Assigning Grades

In the previous chapter, we added a total of five assignments using scales, number grades, outcomes, a marking guide, and a rubric. We also added a graded item directly into the Gradebook.

Once graded activities are added to a Moodle course, we need to award grades to students. Some of the activities are graded by Moodle, such as quizzes and some elements of lessons, but activities with a lot of written content need to be reviewed and graded by the teacher.

In this chapter, we will look at different ways of grading work using a range of grade types. We will see how to:

- Grade assignments with number grades, scales, outcomes, marking guides, and rubrics
- Add written feedback, including inline comments with online text submitted by students
- Download and upload grades using the offline grading options
- Use quick grading directly within the Gradebook

Grading an assignment

Let's first find our way to assignments and the grading screen. Within a course, we need to click on the name of the assignment that we want to grade. If you created the assignments based on the instructions within *Chapter 3*, *Adding Graded Activities*, click on **Task 1** to view it.

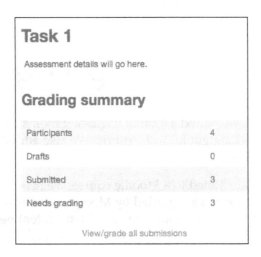

At the top of the assignment screen, we can see the name of the assignment—in this case, **Task 1**—as well as the assignment details. Beneath the assignment details, we are provided with a **Grading summary** section. The grading summary tells us about the following options:

- How many students under the **Participants** option are in the course for which we are expecting assignments to be submitted.

- Beneath this, we can see whether any drafts of work have been submitted in the **Drafts** section.

- The **Submitted** option tells us how many students have submitted their assignment. This is only relevant when students are required to submit their work electronically either through file or an online submission.

- The **Needs grading** option tells us how many of the submitted pieces of assignments need to be graded. This is particularly useful for teachers so that they can quickly see whether they are required to grade any assignment without checking each student submission individually.

Underneath the grading summary, there is the **View/grade all submissions** text. This is a hyperlink that will take us to the assignment grading screen. Click on this link to go into the assignment grading area.

You can see how the grading screen will look in the following screenshot:

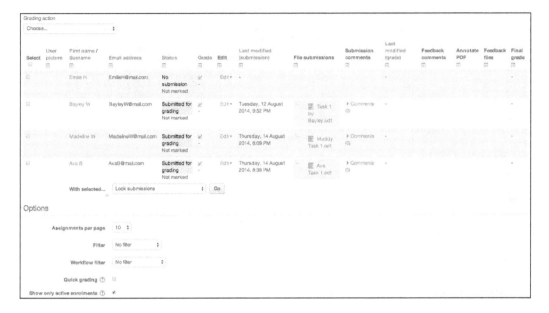

There are three main sections on this page:

- The **Grading action** option is shown at the top of the page. This is a drop-down list through which you can choose to download assignments or select alternative ways of grading.

- The main grading table provides information related to the assessments of each student.

- At the bottom of the assignment grading screen is the **Options** section that enables us to change how we view the assignment grading screen.

There are a lot of options as well as a lot of information on this screen, so we will look at one section at a time. The first area we are going to use is in the central table, as this contains the core information about the assessments for each student. The table starts with the name of each student on the left-hand side, and each column provides different details of student submissions and grades. Each column is explained in the upcoming section.

 Under the title of each column, there is a – symbol that enables a user to hide the content of the column. This is useful in order to provide more usable space. After a column has been collapsed, we will see a + symbol and enable it to expand it again.

In the following screenshot, the **User picture** and **Email address** columns have been minimized in order to show more information:

These columns are explained as follows:

- The first column is a **Select** column where we can choose to select student rows in order to apply actions to them. The options for the selected rows appear beneath the grading table in a drop-down list, as shown in the following screenshot:

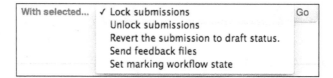

- There are five options to choose from within the list. All the actions within this list can also be undertaken when grading individual assignments, but using the **Select** column and choosing an option from the list allows the action to be applied to multiple students at the same time. After selecting an option, we will click on the **Go** button to complete the action. The five options are explained as follows:

  - **Lock submissions**: This allows a teacher to lock the assignment submissions of selected students in order to prevent them from amending or changing their work while the grading process is taking place.

- ○ **Unlock submissions**: This allows a teacher to unlock assignments in order to enable students to amend or re-upload their work.

- ○ **Revert the submission back to draft status**: This option allows students to resubmit their work.

- ○ **Send feedback files**: This option is only available when file submissions are enabled. The option here allows a teacher to upload feedback files for students. We will be looking at this when grading individual assignments, but this option can be used for a quick upload of feedback files for multiple students.

- ○ **Set marking workflow state**: This option is only relevant when the marking workflow has been turned on when creating the assignment. This enables the teacher to amend the current workflow status of the assignment for multiple students at the same time.

- The next column is the **User picture** column, which is shown in the screenshot as a **+** symbol as this has been minimized. This column, as suggested, shows you the image a student has uploaded as their profile picture. If blind marking has been turned on for the assignment, no column for the user's picture will be shown.

- The **First name/surname** column shows you the student's name at the beginning of each row. If blind marking is turned on for an assignment, a participant number will be shown here instead.

- The **Email address** column shows you the student's email address. In the screenshot, this is shown with a **+** symbol, as this has been minimized.

- The **Status** column shows you the submission and grading status of the assignment of the student. It will indicate whether a student has submitted their assignment (either **No submission** or **Submitted for grading**). It will also show you the grading status (**Not marked** or **Graded**).

- The **Grade** column shows you an icon that is used to access the grading page for a specific student. After the work has been graded, the currently awarded grade will be shown in this column.

- The **Edit** column also enables us to access the assignment grading page as well as perform some quick actions for the assignment. The options will vary depending on the options chosen when creating the assignment and the current status of the assignment. However, the options we are most likely to see are:

  - ○ The **Grade** or **Update grade** option: This takes us to the assignment grading page.

- ° The **Prevent submission changes** option: This enables us to lock a student's submission so that it can no longer be changed.

- ° The **Grant extension** option: This allows the student to submit their assignment after the due date but before the cut-off date. This option is only available if a cut-off date was added when the assignment was created.

- ° The **Edit submission** option: This allows the teacher to upload a file or add online text on behalf of a student. This option is only shown prior to students submitting their own assignment.

- ° The **Revert submission to draft** option: This is shown if students have submitted their assignment but it hasn't been graded yet. Choosing this option will allow the student to submit their assignment again.

- ° The **Allow another attempt** option: This enables the student to have another go at submitting their work. It will enable regrading by the teacher following the submission.

- The next column on the assignment grading table is the **Last modified (submission)** column. This will show you the date and time when the student submitted their work for grading.

- **File submissions** and/or **Online text** will show a link to the file/files that students have uploaded for grading or written into the online text area for submission. Teachers can click to view the files from here, or can view them from the individual grading screen. For assignments with both online and file submissions enabled, there will be two columns.

- **Submission comments** will allow the teacher to view any comments added by students while they were submitting their assignment if this option was turned on within the assignment.

- The **Last modified (grade)** column will show you the date and time when the assignment was graded by a teacher.

- **Feedback comments** will show you the start of any comments given by the teacher after the assignment has been graded.

- If an assignment is submitted as a `.pdf` file, the teacher is given an option to grade it using an integrated editor that allows the teacher to review and annotate the work directly within Moodle. If this option is used for grading, a **View annotated PDF** button will appear within the **Annotate PDF** column.

- **Feedback files** will show you a hyperlink to any files uploaded by the teacher to provide feedback to students. This will only be shown if the **Feedback files** option was selected when creating the assignment.

- The **Final grade** column shows you the grade that was awarded to the student.
- When **Outcomes** are added to an assignment, a column will show you which outcomes are being met by the assignment. Following the grading, this column will show you the grade for each of the outcomes.

There is a lot of information in this table and it provides a good overview of the current status of the assignment for each student.

Some grading can take place from this screen, which we will look at in more detail later, but we will now go to an individual student's grading screen. Click on the **Grade** icon in the **Status** column next to the student you want to grade (make sure that you choose a student who has submitted some work). There are three main sections on the individual grading screen. We will look at each one in turn.

The Submission Status section

The **Submission status** section provides a summary of the assignment for this student, including which attempt this piece of work is, the current submission and grading status of the piece of work, the date the work was submitted, and access to any submitted work. The submitted work can be in the form of a hyperlink to a file or the content of the online submission. For the **Task 1** assignment, students were required to submit a file for their work, and we can see from the following screenshot that **Bayley W** has submitted his assignment:

When files are uploaded, the teacher can click on them in order to open them to view the content.

The Grades section

The **Grade** section will enable us to assign a grade and provide feedback to students, as shown in the following screenshot:

The first option is to select the grade for the piece of work. The grade will depend on the type of grade we selected when creating the assignment. For **Task 1**, we selected **scale grade**, so we are provided with a drop-down list from which we can choose our grade. When grading this assignment for the first time, the **Grade** drop-down list will say **No grade**. If this work is being regraded, then the currently assigned grade will be shown in this list.

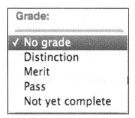

The next option within the **Grade** section is **Marking workflow state**. This will only appear if the marking workflow is turned on when initially setting up the assignment.

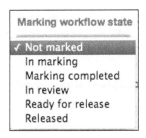

There are six options that the teacher can choose when they are grading the work:

- **Not marked**: This is the state that will be shown prior to grading.

- **In marking**: This will be chosen if the teacher has started grading the assignment but hasn't completed it yet. This option will show other teachers that the grading is still in progress. Students won't be able to view their grade when this option is chosen.

- **Marking completed**: This option will be chosen when the grading is complete, but it should be kept hidden from students. It can be used if a teacher has marked this piece of work but is still grading the work of others.

- **In review**: This option will be used if the initial teacher or assessor has graded the assignment but it needs to undergo a second grading process or needs to be moderated inline along with other work.

- **Ready for release**: This option will be chosen if the work has been graded and reviewed, where appropriate, and is ready for students to view, but we still want to prevent the student from seeing it. This can be used when teachers want to release the assignment to all students at the same time but they are still in the process of grading other work.

- **Released**: This releases the grades and feedback to students and the grade appears within their Gradebook.

The final options within the **Grade** section provide feedback. There were two options that were selected when we created this assignment: **Feedback comments** and **Feedback files**. Within the **Feedback comments** section, we can write feedback for students based on their work. This section has a text editor so that text can be formatted. Within the **Feedback files** section, we can upload files through the **+** icon or drag-and-drop them in order to give more information to students. This could be an annotated copy of the student's original uploaded work, a completed feedback form, or even a sound file that provides audio feedback.

Attempt settings

The final section of the assignment grading screen outlines the current status and some further options for the assignment. The details within this section will vary depending on how the initial assignment was set up. In this example, we opted for attempts to be reopened automatically, so we are only provided with the details of this rather than the option that can change it.

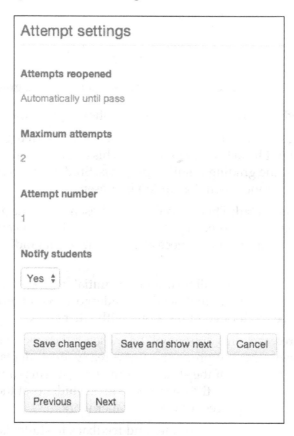

Once each of these sections has been completed, we need to save our work. There are five options at the bottom of the individual grading screen:

- **Save changes**: This enables you to save the grade and feedback and go back to the assignment grading table.

- **Save and show next**: This will save the grade and feedback and move onto the next individual grading page in order to grade another assignment.

- **Cancel**: This will cancel any work completed on the current individual grading screen and show you the assignment grading area.

- **Previous**: This will go to the assignment grading screen of the previous student in the grading list but will not save any work completed on the current grading screen.

- **Next**: This will move on to the next individual grading page but will not save any work completed on the current grading screen.

Once the grading has been completed, you will see that the assignment grading table has been updated. Take a look at **Bayley W** in the following screenshot:

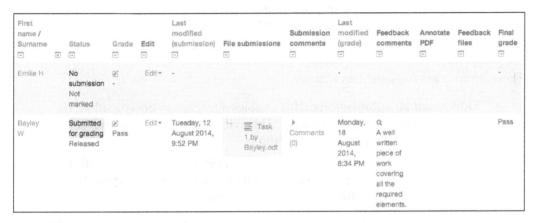

First name / Surname	Status	Grade	Edit	Last modified (submission)	File submissions	Submission comments	Last modified (grade)	Feedback comments	Annotate PDF	Feedback files	Final grade
Emilie H	No submission Not marked	✎ -	Edit ▾	-							
Bayley W	Submitted for grading Released	✎ Pass	Edit ▾	Tuesday, 12 August 2014, 9:52 PM	⊑ ≡ Task 1 by Bayley.odt	▸ Comments (0)	Monday, 18 August 2014, 8:34 PM	🔍 A well written piece of work covering all the required elements.			Pass

All the information regarding the work of **Bayley W** is explained as follows:

- The **Status** column shows you the text, **Submitted for grading** and **Released** which means that not only the work is submitted but has also been released after grading.

- A grade is now shown in the **Grade** column as well as in the **Final grade** column.

- The **Last modified (grade)** column shows you the date and time when the grade was last updated.

- You can see the beginning of the written feedback provided in the **Feedback comments** column. A magnifying glass icon shown in this column enables users to view all the feedback.

When creating the assignment, we enabled offline grading, so let's take a look at how we access this and some of the other grading options available from the grading table page.

Grading options

At the top of the assignment grading table page, there is a drop-down list that provides you with a range of grading options. There are up to five options available in this list but the options will depend on which options were turned on when the assignment was created.

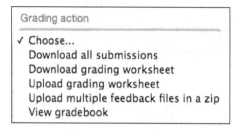

These options are explained as follows:

- **Download all submissions**: This enables a teacher to download all the files uploaded to this assignment. This will create a `.zip` file that can be used to view all the work when offline.

- **Download grading worksheet**: This option is only available if offline grading has been enabled when creating the assignment. It downloads a `.csv` file that contains the assignment information.

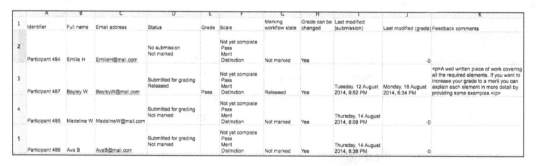

The file contains current information for assignments that are already graded. Take a look at **Bayley W** and note that a grade is already available in column **E** and feedback is shown in column **K**. A teacher can add grades and feedback into this `.csv` file while they are offline, and this can be uploaded to populate the grading table with the relevant grades and feedback.

- **Upload grading worksheet**: We will choose this option if we want to upload the amended grading worksheet.

- **Upload multiple feedback files in a zip**: This option allows students' work to be annotated and re-uploaded as feedback. This works with the **Download all submissions** option. After downloading the files, the folder needs to be unzipped and all files need to be moved to a new folder. The teacher can then review and edit or annotate the files and save them. The file names must not be changed. The new folder can then be zipped and uploaded through this option. This will assign the relevant feedback files to the relevant students.

- **View gradebook**: This option will take us straight to the Gradebook area in order to view all grades for all students.

Options

The **Options** section enables us to customize how the grading table is viewed as well as provide some quick grading options. Individual teachers can customize how they view the assignment grading area. Three main options are shown at the bottom of the assignment grading screen.

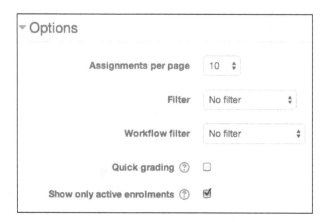

These options are explained as follows:

- **Assignments per page**: This option allows us to choose how many rows of students are shown per page. For example, if we have 12 students in the course, we can choose to view all 12 on one screen rather than move to another screen to review the final two students. Alternatively, if students are submitting many files per assignment, we might only want to view one or two students per page so that we can see all the information easily on the screen.

- **Filter**: This is a very useful drop-down list on the grading table that only shows you the assignments that we need to consider:
    - **Not submitted**: This only shows you students who have not submitted any work
    - **Submitted**: This only shows you students who have submitted an assignment
    - **Requires grading**: This option will only show you any assignment that is currently ungraded

- **Workflow filter**: This option allows a teacher to choose to view only students within a specific part of the workflow. This can be useful to move multiple students through the workflow process.

- **Quick grading**: A tick in this box will give you an alternative way to grade a student's work. Let's look at this in more detail.

Quick grading within the assignment grading screen

Turning on the **Quick grading** option turns the assignment grading area into an editable table that will enable us to add a grade and some written feedback directly onto the screen without needing to enter individual student pages. Quick grading is very useful for offline activities or assignments that have already been viewed offline. When a tick is added to the **Quick grading** box, three columns are changed.

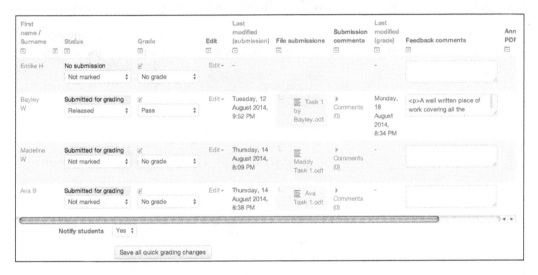

- The **Status** column includes a drop-down list that changes the workflow phase for the student (if the marking workflow is turned on for the assignment).

- The **Grade** column also has a drop-down list next to each student in order to enable us to choose the grade that we would like to award. This is the same drop-down list as the one on the individual grading screen and will show you all the options within the scale. If this assignment were to be graded with a number, an empty text box would appear here in order to enable us to type in the grade to be awarded.

- The **Feedback comments** column also has a text entry box that enables us to type in some feedback for the assignment. The feedback box can be made larger with the resizing area in the bottom-right section of the box, but there is no editor to change how the information looks.

Once all the grades and written feedback have been added, it is important that you click on **Save all quick grading changes** at the bottom of the grading table in order to save the completed feedback. We have now seen most of the main features and functions of the assignment grading table. However, we created a range of different type of assignments, so let's take a look at how we can grade other grade types.

Grading an online text assignment with a number grade

When creating assignments in *Chapter 3, Adding Graded Activities*, we created **Task 2** in order to enable students to submit text online, and the maximum grade possible was set to **20**. View Task 2 to follow the instructions for the grading process.

As with the previous assignment, we are initially provided with **Grading summary**, and we need to click on **View/grade all assignments**. This will open up the assignment grading table.

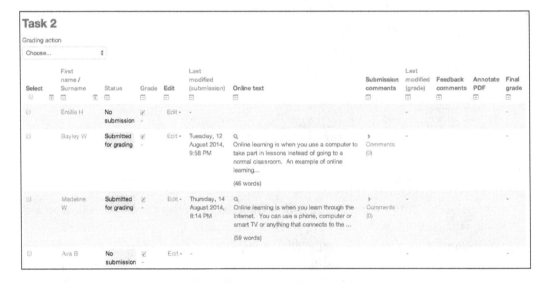

The grading table is similar to the one we have already used, but on this table, we have an **Online text** column instead of a **File submissions** column. Take a look at your grading table and choose a student who has the **Submitted for grading** text in the **Status** column. Click on the **grading** icon within the **Grade** column next to the student's name.

As shown previously, the page begins with some information about the **Submission status** section. Much of this information is the same as what was used previously, but take note of the **Online text** information shown on this page. This will allow you to read the assignment submitted by the student. In most cases, there will be more text than can be seen on this screen, so a **+** symbol is shown for us to expand the information in order to read the full submission.

Submission status

Attempt number	This is attempt 1.
Submission status	Submitted for grading
Grading status	Not graded
Editing status	Student cannot edit this submission
Last modified	Thursday, 14 August 2014, 8:14 PM
Online text	⊞ Online learning is when you learn through the internet. You can use a phone, computer or smart TV or anything that connects to the ... (59 words)
Submission comments	▸ Comments (0)

In the **Submission status** section, we have the **Grade** section, which begins with the option to assign a grade. For the previous assignment, we graded assignments with a scale that provided a drop-down list for us to choose the grade. As this assignment is a number grade, we are provided with a text entry box instead and are informed to assign a grade in the **Grade out of 20** option. We are not likely to complete this until we have reviewed the work but when we are ready, we simply need to type in a number between 0 and 20 in order to assign a grade to the assignment.

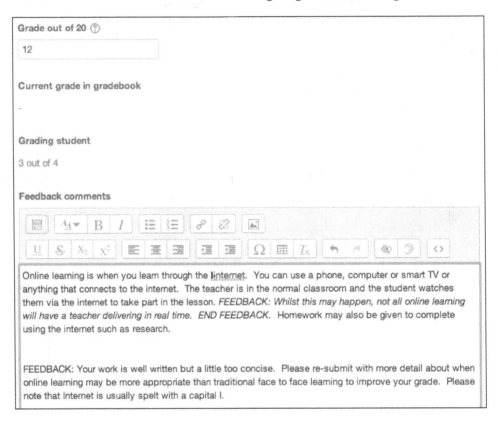

Toward the bottom of this section, we can see that the **Feedback comments** box already has some text in it. This text is the assignment submitted by the student. This information appears in the box, as we selected **Comment inline** when we initially created the assignment. We can edit this text and add further information in order to provide feedback to the students. We will need to make our feedback stand out from the student's original text, so we will need to make use of the text editor that is available at the top of the **Feedback comments** box.

Click on **Save changes** to submit the feedback and grade to the Gradebook and inform the student.

So far, we have graded assignments with a scale and number and have viewed assignments submitted as a file and online text. When creating assignments, we also set up a third task, which is **Task 3**, that makes use of all of these and utilizes the **Outcomes** feature. Let's take a look now at how to grade outcomes.

Grading an assignment with outcomes

After viewing the assignment and clicking on **View/grade all assignments**, we will see the assignment grading table. As this assignment has enabled **File submissions** and **Online text** submissions, both of these columns appear in the table. As we have added outcomes to this assignment, there is an additional column at the end of the grading table, which shows you the outcomes that are used.

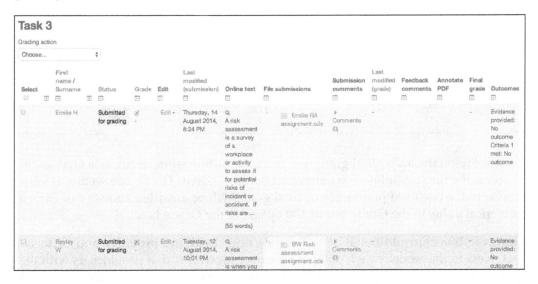

Note that currently, the text **No outcome** appears with each outcome. This shows you that the assignments haven't been graded yet.

We will use the individual grading screen to grade the outcomes, so we need to click on the **grade** icon in the **Grade** column next to the student whose work we want to mark.

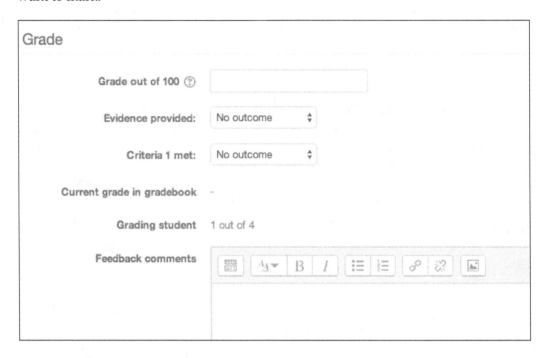

Once we're on the individual grading screen, the **Submission status** area enables us to access the file and online text submitted by the student. The **Grade** section is very similar to the one used previously. A final grade will be awarded and we can enter a numerical value in the **Grade out of 100** option in the **Grade** box.

However, there are additional items to grade now: **Evidence provided** and **Criteria 1 met**. Next to the name of each outcome is a drop-down list that provides us with the scale chosen when setting up the outcomes. To grade each outcome, we need to click on the drop-down list in order to choose the grade we want to provide.

The other option we turned on for this assignment, which we haven't seen in practice yet, is the option to manually reopen an assignment in order to enable resubmission. This option is within the **Attempt settings** section.

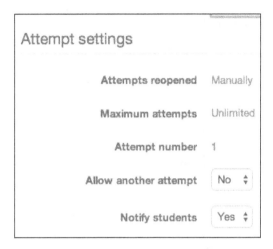

If we want to enable the student to resubmit their work again, we need to change the **Allow another attempt** option to **Yes** using the drop-down list.

When grading all assignments, we need to ensure that we click on **Save changes** when we have added the grades and feedback.

We have now looked at all the key options when grading assignments with the simple direct grading method, and we have also created assignments using the advanced grading methods that utilize the marking guide and rubric grading tools. Let's take a look at how to grade these assignments.

Grading an assignment with a marking guide

If you followed the instructions in *Chapter 3*, *Adding Graded Activities*, open the assignment titled **Assignment 4**.

The assignment grading table will be the same as the one we have seen previously with the simple grading method, Click on **View/grade all submissions** and click on the grade icon next to a student that you want to grade.

The biggest difference between the grading pages we have seen previously and using the marking guide is the way in which we grade the assignment. When grading assignments with a scale, we were provided with a drop-down list in order to add the grade, and for a numerical grade, we had a textbox to which we could type the grade. For a marking guide assignment, there is no single grade entry point. Instead, we are provided with the grading criteria for which we can add a grade. Moodle will then add each grade together in order to provide the final grade for the assignment.

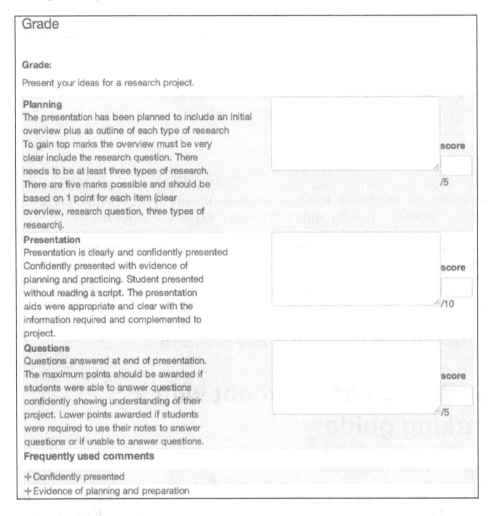

Next to each piece of criteria, there is a text entry box and a score box. Take a look at the previous screenshot and find the criteria titled **Planning**. The **Grade** section is explained as follows:

- We can see the full details of the criteria that aids us by providing us with the correct grade.

- To the right of this criteria, we have a textbox where we can add feedback in relation to this criteria. When creating this assignment, we also added some comments in the **Frequently used comments** option, and we can see these at the bottom of the marking guide. If we would like to add any of these comments to the feedback, we need to click on the box where we want to add the comment and then click on the **+** symbol next to the frequently used comment that we want to use.

- The final column on the right-hand side provides a grade entry box. Underneath this box, we can see the maximum number of points that are available for this criteria. To provide a grade, we add a number grade up to the given maximum grade.

Like the simple grading methods, we also have the option to add general feedback, and we can also have options to change the marking workflow and reopen submissions depending on how the assignment was set up.

After adding the feedback and individual criteria grades, we need to click on the **Save changes** button.

Following the grading, each score assigned to each piece of criteria is added together in order to provide the final grade for the student, and this can be seen in the **Grade** column in the assignment grading table.

Bayley W	Submitted for grading Graded	15.00 / 20.00

The student will see the final grade and each individual criteria grade and feedback when reviewing the feedback for their assignment.

The final type of grading that we set up in *Chapter 3, Adding Graded Activities*, was through the use of a rubric. Grading with a rubric is similar to using a marking guide. Let's take a look at this together.

Grading an assignment with a rubric

If you created **Assignment 5**, click to view this now and make your way to the grading screen of a selected student. Much like the marking guide, instead of a single grade entry point, we have a table that provides us with the criteria for the assignment. However, unlike the marking guide, we will not be grading with a numerical grade of our choice.

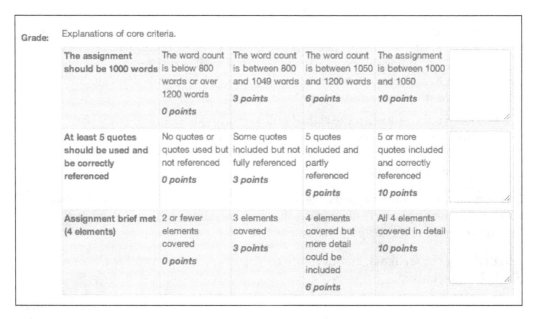

Grade:	Explanations of core criteria.					
The assignment should be 1000 words	The word count is below 800 words or over 1200 words 0 points	The word count is between 800 and 1049 words 3 points	The word count is between 1050 and 1200 words 6 points	The assignment is between 1000 and 1050 10 points	
At least 5 quotes should be used and be correctly referenced	No quotes or quotes used but not referenced 0 points	Some quotes included but not fully referenced 3 points	5 quotes included and partly referenced 6 points	5 or more quotes included and correctly referenced 10 points	
Assignment brief met (4 elements)	2 or fewer elements covered 0 points	3 elements covered 3 points	4 elements covered but more detail could be included 6 points	All 4 elements covered in detail 10 points	

The rubric table enables us to easily grade work even though there is a lot of information on the screen.

When grading assignments, the teacher reviews the work and clicks on the box that contains the statement and points that they want to award. We can also add written feedback in the textbox on each row. A section to add in the overall feedback is also available.

In the following screenshot, you can see how this rubric grid has been completed by the teacher:

Grade:	Explanations of core criteria.				
The assignment should be 1000 words	The word count is below 800 words or over 1200 words 0 points	The word count is between 800 and 1049 words 3 points	The word count is between 1050 and 1200 words 6 points	The assignment is between 1000 and 1050 10 points	Word count 1119
At least 5 quotes should be used and be correctly referenced	No quotes or quotes used but not referenced 0 points	Some quotes included but not fully referenced 3 points	5 quotes included and partly referenced 6 points	5 or more quotes included and correctly referenced 10 points	You need to check your referencing and update your work.
Assignment brief met (4 elements)	2 or fewer elements covered 0 points	3 elements covered 3 points	4 elements covered but more detail could be included 6 points	All 4 elements covered in detail 10 points	Excellent work.

The shaded boxes show you the grade awarded for each criterion, and some comments have been added to the feedback column as well.

The final grade for the assignment is calculated by Moodle by adding together each of the points awarded within the rubric, and this is shown in the assignment grading table within the Grade column.

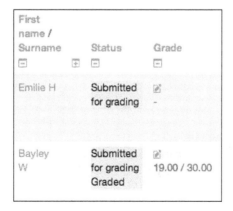

As with the marking guide, the student will see the full rubric table and comments when they receive their assignment feedback.

Grading a graded item within the Gradebook

We have seen how we can grade assignments by accessing the activities from within the main course screen. However, in *Chapter 3, Adding Graded Activities*, we also added a graded activity directly into the Gradebook. So, how do we grade this? We go into the Gradebook! Let's take a look:

1. From the main course screen, go to the **Grades** area (navigate to **Administration | Grades**).

2. Click on the **Turn editing on** button in the top-right corner of the screen.

3. We will be able to add a grade directly into the graded item.

In the previous screenshot, you can see the **Attendance grade** option. This item was set up as a value grade. To add the grade, we type a number into the empty textbox. At the bottom of the screen, there is an **Update** button that saves any grades that we have added.

We can also use this grading method for any other type of graded activity within the Gradebook.

Quick grading within the Gradebook

Turning editing on within the **Grades** area will allow us to grade any graded activity.

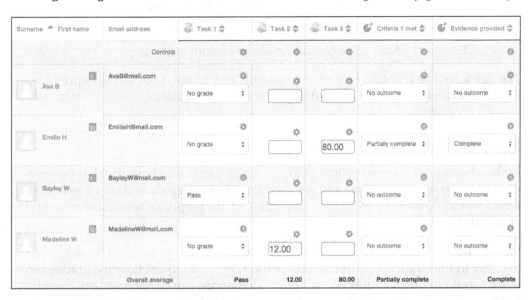

In the previous screenshot, we can see different types of grades. **Task 1** is an example of an assignment that is graded with a scale and, therefore, quick grading provides a drop-down list that enables us to choose the grade we would like to award. **Task 2** and **Task 3**, however, have been set as numerical grades, so we need to type the number into the grade box. Also, as part of **Task 3**, there are two columns that show you outcomes that are graded using a drop-down list that chooses a scale item.

After we have amended grades on this screen, we need to click on the **Update** button to save the grades.

There are a few things to consider when using quick grading:

- We cannot see the maximum grade when adding number grades.
- The marking guide and rubric-graded assignments cannot be marked via the quick grading option.

When using the quick grading option, we can choose to add quick feedback, but this option is not shown on the current screen. However, we can change some settings to enable this:

1. Click on the **My preferences** tab, or click on **Grader report** under the **My preferences** heading.
2. Scroll to the **General** section at the bottom of the page.
3. Next to the **Show quick feedback** text, change the drop-down list to **Yes**.
4. Click on the **Save changes** button at the bottom of the page.

The quick feedback option is limited to adding text, so if a lot of text is required, it is recommended that the individual grading screen be used.

Summary

In this chapter, we have seen how to grade assignments that have number or scale grades and graded outcomes, and we used the marking guide and rubric grading forms. We also saw how we can use the quick grading options within the assignment area and the Gradebook screen.

We saw how we can grade individual assignments, but how do all of these come together in the Gradebook? In the next chapter, we will look at how the grades can work together in the Gradebook and how calculations can be set up to calculate the final course grades. We will also see how we can further customize the Gradebook.

5
Using Calculations

In this chapter, you will learn about the various options and settings available to calculate and display a final grade in the Gradebook. We will also look at the options available when choosing how the grades are displayed. In this chapter, we will cover the following sections:

- How grades are calculated
- Using a range of preset aggregations to calculate course totals
- Changing how grades are shown in the Gradebook

Calculating the course grade

All graded activities that are added to the online course will automatically be added to the Gradebook. Students can have a range of assessments for which they will be given a range of scores. Apart from storing these grades, the Gradebook can also calculate a final grade based on a range of preset aggregation settings available within the course. Aggregation means to bring together all the scores and then perform a calculation to present a final grade.

Before this aggregation takes place, a normalization process happens. Normalization is when the grade given to an individual assessment is converted into a decimal for the calculations.

Why use normalization?

Normalization is required in order to ensure that all the grades have the same base value so that they can be calculated fairly in relation to the maximum grade. For example, a grade of 20 out of 100 is a lower percentage score than 20 out of 20, so using both scores as 20 would not accurately represent the real achievement of the student.

For the Gradebook to calculate a fair total, we need both of the grades to be recalculated to a decimal so that they have the same base value prior to adding them together for the final course grade. The calculation of normalization is the grade awarded, divided by the total grade possible so that all the graded activities have a base value of 10. The following table shows this for the two activities in this example:

	Graded activity 1	Graded activity 2
Maximum grade possible	20	100
Grade awarded	20	20
Grade following normalization	1.0	0.2

As you can see, the normalized grade now shows that the two awarded scores of 20 should not be treated the same when calculating the final course grade as they have significantly different decimal scores. This is this score that is used in the aggregation process.

We will see many more examples of how this normalization process is used as we complete examples throughout the chapter and see how the different aggregation types use the normalized grades.

Aggregation types

Moodle has a range of aggregation types available, and these are outlined briefly in the upcoming section. These are shown in the order in which they are listed within Moodle. The ones shown in bold are some of the most popular or more complex to understand so will be used as detailed examples later in the chapter, and the actual calculations will be explained in more detail. However, for each aggregation type, quick examples will also be given to show the calculation that takes place. For all the examples, the normalized grades of 1.0 and 0.2, as shown in the previous example, will be used:

- The **mean of grades**: Following normalization, the average score is calculated as the final score by adding up the total grades awarded and dividing it by the total number of graded items, for example, *(1.0 + 0.2)/2=0.6*.

- The **weighted mean of grades**: Each graded item can be given a weight. The grade given for the assessed item is normalized and then multiplied by the item's weight to create an increased item grade. The final grade is calculated by adding together the increased item grades and then dividing them by the total weights applied (for example, if two assessments are given a x2 weight, the total of the increased grades added together will be divided by four). In this example, graded item one will be given a weighting of x2 and graded item two will be given a weighting of x3: *(1.0x2)+(0.2x3)/5=0.52*.

- The **simple weighted mean of grades**: This is the default aggregation method when no settings have been changed within the Gradebook. In this version of the weighted mean type, the maximum grades of each assessed item are used as the weighting instead of the teacher needing to apply separate weights to each graded activity. For example, one assessed activity could be graded out of 100 and another activity could be graded out of 50. The first graded item would be worth more to the final course total than the second. Again, the Gradebook first normalizes the grade and then multiplies that grade by the total grade possible. These increased assessment activity grades are then divided by the total weight possible (that is, the total of all the maximum grades in the course), for example, *(1.0x20)+(0.2x100)/120=0.333*.

- The **mean of grades (with extra credit)**: This aggregation type is only available in Moodle to enable upgraded courses that already use this aggregation type to continue to use it (that is, for backwards compatibility). Instead, the weighted and simple weighted mean options should be used to prevent the use of an aggregation method that is no longer supported .Where this aggregation is still used, it is possible to apply an extra credit grade that can be added to the final mean grade. Any item with no extra credit applied will be used as part of the final mean calculation. However, items with extra credit applied will be added to the final total in addition to the mean grade. For our example, we will add an additional graded item with the score of 1.0, but this will be given extra credit of 2.0. The other two grades will not have any extra credit applied, so the mean calculation will apply to these. In this example, the mean grade — *(1.0 + 0.2)/2=0.6* — is added to the extra credit grade *(1.0x2)=2.0*. The final grade is 2.6.

- The **median of grades**: All the normalized grades are put into a numerical order from the lowest to the highest, and the final grade will be the grade in the middle of this list. If there is no middle number (if the total number of grades is an even number), Moodle will take the two middle numbers and present the average grade of these two as the final grade. For example, as there are only two numbers in our example, the final course grade will be an average — *(1.0+02)/2=0.6*. An additional graded item will be included as an example. This grade will be 30 out of 30, which will provide a normalized grade of 1.0. Therefore, there are now three grades for this example: 0.2, 1.0, and 1.0, which are shown in a lowest to highest order. The Gradebook will present the final grade as 1.0, as this is the grade in the middle.

- The **lowest grade**: This reviews all the grades after normalization and presents the lowest score as the final grade. For example, the final grade will be 0.2.

- The **highest grade**: This reviews all the grades after normalization and presents the highest score as the final grade. For example, the final grade will be 1.0.

- The **mode of grades**: Following normalization, the Gradebook reviews all the grades and the grade that is awarded most frequently is presented as the final grade, for example, 0.2, 1.0, and 1.0. The final grade is 1.0.

- **Sum of grades**: This is the only aggregation method that does not use normalization. In this aggregation type, the Gradebook simply adds together each score awarded for each assessment. This maximum grade possible for the course is the sum of all the maximum grades possible for each individual assessment added together, for example, $20 + 20 = 40$ out of a maximum grade of 120.

Maximum grades

It is possible to set a maximum score for the course, which means that Moodle will calculate the final score based on that maximum grade.

For example, 10 assessments in a course, each with a maximum grade of 25, will have a course total of 250. However, the final course grade achievable might only be 100. Therefore, the aggregation process can also convert the final score so that it is graded out of 100 (rather than 250).

Where a maximum score is applied, the Gradebook will add an additional calculation after the aggregation, as shown in the following step 3. Therefore, the full aggregation process will be as follows:

1. Normalize grades.
2. Calculate the aggregation (for example, apply weights, add grades together, calculate the average, and so on).
3. Multiply the aggregated normalized grades by the course maximum grade.

 Maximum grades do not apply to the sum of grades aggregation.

Confused? Let's take a look at an example to see the normalization, aggregation, and maximum grade calculations in action! Take a look at the following table and note the formulas shown in brackets to see the processes that the Gradebook is completing for us.

In this example, there are five graded activities within the course, each with a different maximum grade possible. The Gradebook aggregation is set as a calculation of the mean of grades (the average of the grades). The maximum grade possible for the whole course is 100. The shaded row is the information that the Gradebook uses for the aggregation/calculations.

Assignment	A1	A2	A3	A4	A5	Usual total	Mean aggregation	Final grade shown in the Gradebook
Max grade possible	25	50	40	25	20	160	32	
Grade awarded	20	35	38	25	15	133	26.6	
Normalized grade (a)	0.8 (20/25)	0.7 (35/50)	0.95 (38/40)	1 (25/25)	0.75 (15/20)	4.2 (b) (.8+.7+.95+1+.75)	0.84 (4.2/5)	84 (c) (.84*100)

The preceding table can be explained as follows:

- **(a)**: To calculate the normalized grade, the grade awarded is divided by the maximum grade for each assignment.

- **(b)**: The mean aggregation grade is calculated by adding together the normalized grade for each of the grade items. This is then divided by five (the total number of grades awarded).

- **(c)**: The final grade is 84 as the mean aggregation grade is multiplied by 100, which is the course maximum. If the course maximum was 30, the final grade would be *25.2 (0.84*30=25.2)*.

Let's go into the Gradebook and set up some examples to see the aggregation types in action and learn some other things that we can do to customize the Gradebook so that it can further meet our needs.

Example one – The mean of grades

In this example, three assignments have been added to the Moodle course. Two have a maximum grade of 100 and one has a maximum grade of 50. If you want to follow the instructions to set up an example Gradebook, create three assignments and choose 100 as the maximum grade for **Task 1** and **Task 2** and 50 for **Task 3**. Grade **Task 1** and **Task 2** for at least one learner. In the following example, you can see activities we use:

Surname ▲ First name			Email address	Task 1 ⬍	Task 2 ⬍	Task 3 ⬍
	Ava B		AvaB@mail.com	94.00	-	-
	Emilie H		EmilieH@mail.com	99.00	-	-
	Bayley W		BayleyW@mail.com	91.00	100.00	-
	Madeline W		MadelineW@mail.com	86.00	100.00	-

The aggregation type of this course will be the mean of grades, which will present a final average grade.

Let's go into the **Grades** area and choose the aggregation type:

1. Click on the **Administration** block and then click on **Grades**.

   You should see a table like the previous one, which will show you the grades of each assignment for each student. If you see an overall average row at the bottom of the screen, don't let it confuse you. This is an average grade based on all the students in the course rather than an individual student's average grade, and it is shown for all aggregation types. You will learn more about customizing this screen in *Chapter 7, Reporting with the Gradebook*.

2. From the drop-down list at the top of the screen, find **Categories and items** and choose **Simple view** (or click on the **Categories and items** tab if your screen shows the tabs view).

This is where we can start to customize the Gradebook and choose the aggregation type.

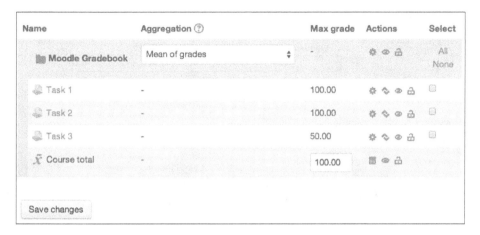

You can see that the **categories and items** screen is another table with column headings that explain the content of the table. You can change the aggregation of the course from the drop-down list in the aggregation column. Click on the drop-down list box and choose **Mean of grades**, then click on **Save changes** at the bottom of the screen. This is not the only way to change the aggregation type, and we will look at other ways of doing this later in the chapter.

Take a look at the **Max grade** column. This shows you the maximum grade possible for each graded item in the course and the course total, which is the number at the bottom of the table, shows you the total final grade possible. In this example, the course total is displayed as 100 as this is the default (except for the sum of grades aggregation type), but it can be easily changed by typing an alternative number into this course total box.

Let's switch back to view the Gradebook. In the drop-down list at the top of the screen, find **View** icon and click on **Grader report** (or click on **View** on the tab at the top of the Gradebook screen).

Before we look at other customizations possible, let's take a quick look at how the aggregation will work in this example. Remember, for this example, we are using the mean of grades aggregation type, and this type of calculation converts the grades to a normalized score, adds them all together, and divides this normalized total by the total number of graded items in the course. Finally, this is multiplied by the course total—in this case, 100—to provide the final score.

Take a look at the following screenshot and you can see the **Course total** that shows you the mean grade for each student:

Surname ▲ First name		Email address	Task 1 ⇕	Task 2 ⇕	Task 3 ⇕	𝑋̃ Course total ⇕
	Ava B	AvaB@mail.com	94.00	-	-	94.00
	Emilie H	EmilieH@mail.com	99.00	-	-	99.00
	Bayley W	BayleyW@mail.com	91.00	100.00	-	95.50
	Madeline W	MadelineW@mail.com	86.00	100.00	-	93.00
		Overall average	**92.50**	**100.00**	**-**	**95.38**

Take a look at the information of **Bayley W**, who has completed two assessments that have been graded. His current course total is **95.50**, which could be this calculation: *91.00 + 100.00 / 2* (that is, the two assignment grades added together and divided by the total number of grades added together). However, this only works because the course total is the same as the assignment maximum grades. If the course total was 50, we could not have performed this simple calculation for the course total. This is why Moodle first normalizes grades and then multiplies this by the maximum course total possible. So, the calculation that Moodle is actually doing for **Bayley W** is shown in the following table:

	Task 1	Task 2	Total	Mean aggregation	Final grade shown in the Gradebook
Maximum grade possible	100	100			
Grade awarded	91.00	100.00	191	95.50	
Normalized grade	0.91 (91/100)	1 (100/100)	1.91 (0.91+1)	0.955 (1.91/2)	95.50 (.0955*100)

As you can see, only the assessments that have actually been graded are included in the aggregation for the course total. So, the student is given a current grade based on work that has already been completed. However, what if you want to provide a running total? What if you want the students to know the final grade they will get based on the work completed to date even if it is not complete yet? This is particularly important if all assignments need to be completed in order to complete the course and gain a final grade.

Including all graded activities

We can tell the Gradebook to include all the graded activities in the aggregation. Moodle will add up each assessed activity, which will include a zero score for each assessed item that has not been submitted or graded yet, and then it will divide the grade by the total number of assessed grades in the course regardless of whether they have been graded or not. In this example, it will be divided by three. Let's go and apply this and see it in action:

1. Go to **Categories and items** again (either by clicking on the drop-down list and clicking on **Simple view** under the **categories and items** heading or by clicking on **Categories and items** in the tabs bar).

2. In the top row in the **Actions** column (in the same row as the aggregation drop-down list), the first icon is an edit icon (a cog icon for the default Moodle theme; if you hold your mouse over the first icon, it will give you a screen tip that says edit). Click on the edit icon.

We are only going to use the **Grade category** section for now. However, the options that we need are not shown on the screen so we need to click on **Show more**:

Note that you can change the aggregation method on this screen. However, the setting we need to change is the **Aggregate only non-empty grades** option. Notice that this box is currently checked. Click on the box to remove the tick and scroll to the bottom of the screen to go to **Save changes**.

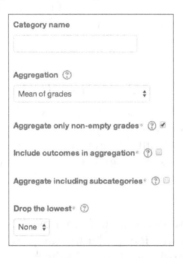

 This option can be applied with any aggregation type (except the sum of grades) by clicking on the edit icon in the **Actions** column on the **Categories and items** screen.

Let's take a look at the Gradebook again to see what difference this has made. (To go back to the Gradebook, use the drop-down list at the top of the screen, find **View**, and click on **Grader report** or click on **View** in the tab at the top of the Gradebook screen.)

Surname ▲ First name		Email address	Task 1 ⬍	Task 2 ⬍	Task 3 ⬍	$\bar{X}$ Course total ⬍
Ava B		AvaB@mail.com	94.00	-	-	31.33
Emilie H		EmilieH@mail.com	99.00	-	-	33.00
Bayley W		BayleyW@mail.com	91.00	100.00	-	63.67
Madeline W		MadelineW@mail.com	86.00	100.00	-	62.00
		Overall average	92.50	100.00	-	47.50

You can see that the course total has now changed as it is including all the graded items in the aggregation. The fewer items that have been marked the lower the grade will be. The calculation that is taking place for **Bayley W** is now as follows:

	Task 1	Task 2	Task 3	Total	Mean aggregation	Final grade shown in Gradebook
Max grade possible	100	100	50			
Grade awarded	91.00	100.00	0	191	63.67	
normalized grade	0.91 (91/100)	1 (100/100)	0 (0/50)	1.91 (0.91+1+0)	0.6367 (1.91/3)	63.67 (.06367*100)

We have been using the mean of grades, but there are two other mean aggregation types.

Let's keep using this example but change the Gradebook to show **Simple weighted mean of grades** and the **Weighted mean of grades** to see how they affect the final aggregation. This will also give us the chance to practice how to change aggregation types within the course.

The simple weighted mean of grades

In the mean of the grades aggregation type that we have been using, the totals for each assignment type are not taken into consideration in the final aggregation (other than for the normalization process). It is only the grades that are used. However, in the simple weighted mean of the grades aggregation type, the maximum grade of each assignment is very important. This aggregation type uses the assignment totals in the mean aggregation step of the calculation.

Let's change the aggregation of the course and see what it does to the final grade:

1. Go to **Categories and items** again (either by clicking on the drop-down list and clicking on **Simple view** under the **categories and items** heading, or by clicking on **Categories and items** in the tabs bar).

2. Change the aggregation type to **Simple weighted mean of grades** with the drop-down list in the **Aggregation** column, and click on **Save changes** at the bottom of the screen.

3. Now, switch back to view the Gradebook. On the drop-down list at the top of the screen, find **View** and click on **Grader report** (or click on **View** on the tab at the top of the Gradebook screen).

Note how the course total score has changed. Look at **Bayley W** again. His previous score in the mean of grades aggregation was **63.67** (remember that the Gradebook is currently using all the assessed activities in the calculations and not just those that have been marked and graded). His score is **76.40** now.

Surname ▲ First name	Email address	🖼 Task 1 ⬍	🖼 Task 2 ⬍	🖼 Task 3 ⬍	𝑋̄ Course total ⬍
Ava B 📧	AvaB@mail.com	94.00	-	-	37.60
Emilie H 📧	EmilieH@mail.com	99.00	-	-	39.60
Bayley W 📧	BayleyW@mail.com	91.00	100.00	-	76.40
Madeline W 📧	MadelineW@mail.com	86.00	100.00	-	74.40
	Overall average	92.50	100.00	-	57.00

The calculation used in the simple weighted mean of grades is shown in the following table:

	Task 1	Task 2	Task 3	Total	Mean aggregation	Final grade shown in the Gradebook
Maximum grade possible	100	100	50	250		
Grade awarded	91.00	100.00	0	191	63.67	
Normalized grade	0.91 (91/100)	1 (100/100)	0 (0/50)	1.91 (.91+1+0)		
Plus weighting	91 (.91*100)	100 (1*100)	0 (0*50)	191 (91+100+0)	.764 (191/250)	76.40 (.764*100)

As done previously, the grade awarded is normalized. However, in this aggregation method, this normalized grade is multiplied by the maximum grade possible for the assessed activity. (In theory, the normalization process is not required in this aggregation type, as the normalization and weighting calculations cancel each other back to the original grade awarded. However, in practice, Moodle always normalizes this aggregation type.) However, the calculation of the mean aggregation is different in this method.

Instead of dividing the normalized total by the number of grades in the course (in our example, this meant dividing the total by three), the simple weighted mean aggregation divides the normalized total by the total maximum grade possible (which is each of the maximum grades for each activity added together). In this case, it divides the normalized and weighted total by 250.

There is one final method of calculating a mean grade and this requires some additional options to be set by the teacher. Let's have a go at using the 'weighted mean of grades' aggregation method.

The weighted mean of grades

In this method, each graded item in the course is manually given a weighting. In the mean of grades method, there is no weighting involved as it is a simple average calculation. In the simple weighted mean of grades, the weighting is based on the maximum grade possible for each graded item. In a weighted mean, the teacher sets the weighting within the Gradebook. An example use of this aggregation type is when a specific assignment is worth more to the final course grade than others. For example, in our sample activities, **Task 1** and **Task 2** both have a maximum grade of 100. However, **Task 2** might require a lot more detail and research to complete the task and therefore, it should contribute more to the final grade than **Task 1**. With the simple weighted mean aggregation type, the two tasks will be treated equally. However, we can reflect the additional work within the final grade by making use of the weighting option within the weighted mean of grades:

1. Go to **Categories and items** again.
2. Change the **Aggregation** type to **Weighted mean of grades**.

   There are further changes that now need to be made here. Once the weighted mean of grades has been chosen, a new column appears on the **Categories and items** page. This is the **Weight** column and it allows us to apply a weight to each graded item. The default for each item is **1.0**. However, in this example, **Task 2** has been changed to a weighting of two in order to reflect the additional work required when completing this activity.

 You can also use the weighted mean of grades to exclude a grade from the course total. To do this, we will need to change the weighting to **0.0**.

3. Change the weighting of **Task 2** to **2.0** and click on **Save changes** at the bottom of the screen.

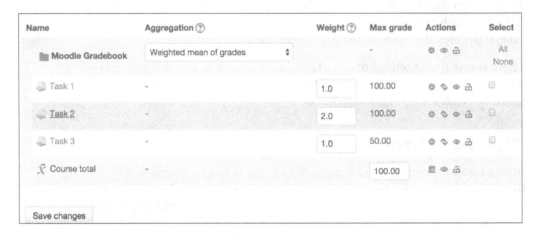

Name	Aggregation ⑦	Weight ⑦	Max grade	Actions	Select
📔 Moodle Gradebook	Weighted mean of grades ⬍	-		⚙ 👁 🔒	All None
🔲 Task 1	-	1.0	100.00	⚙ 🔷 👁 🔒	☐
🔲 Task 2	-	2.0	100.00	⚙ 🔷 👁 🔒	☐
🔲 Task 3	-	1.0	50.00	⚙ 🔷 👁 🔒	☐
𝑋̄ Course total	-		100.00	🔲 👁 🔒	

Save changes

Let's see how this affects the final grade:

*   Switch back to view the Gradebook. In the drop-down list at the top of the screen, find **View** and click on **Grader report** (or click on **view** in the tab at the top of the Gradebook screen).

Surname ▲ First name		Email address	🔲 Task 1 ⬍	🔲 Task 2 ⬍	🔲 Task 3 ⬍	𝑋̄ Course total ⬍
Ava B	🔳	AvaB@mail.com	94.00	-	-	23.50
Emilie H	🔳	EmilieH@mail.com	99.00	-	-	24.75
Bayley W	🔳	BayleyW@mail.com	91.00	100.00	-	72.75
Madeline W	🔳	MadelineW@mail.com	86.00	100.00	-	71.50
		Overall average	92.50	100.00	-	48.13

The course totals have changed again, so let's see how this is calculated. In this method of calculating a mean grade, each normalized grade is multiplied by the weight applied to the assessed item. The normalized grades are added together and then divided by the total weights applied to the course. The following table shows you the calculations for this aggregation method for the grades of **Bayley W**:

	Task 1	Task 2	Task 3	Total	Mean aggregation	Final grade shown in the Gradebook
Maximum grade possible	100	100	50			
Grade awarded	91.00	100.00	0	191	63.67	
Weighting	1	2	1		Total: 4	
Normalized grade	0.91 (91/100*1)	2 (100/100*2)	0 (0/50*1)	2.91 (0.91+2+0)	0.7275 (1.91/4)	72.75 (.7275*100)

Note that **Task 2** is multiplied by two as this is the weighting we applied for this assessed activity. The mean aggregation is calculated by dividing the total weighted normalized score by four, as this is the total number of weights applied to the course (that is, a weighting of one for **Task 1**, a weighting of two for **Task 2**, and a weighting of one for **Task 3**).

We have seen three ways of how to calculate a mean grade within a course and customize the Gradebook by choosing to include all assessed activities within the Gradebook rather than just the graded activities. Another popular aggregation method is the sum of grades, which acts differently to the normalized methods already discussed. Let's have a go with this aggregation method. We will also look at some other customizations available in order to change how the grade is displayed within the Gradebook.

Example two – The sum of grades

In this example, we will look at the 'sum of grades' aggregation type. The course has five assignments for the students to complete, each with a different final grade.

With the following screenshot, you can see how this example course has been set up:

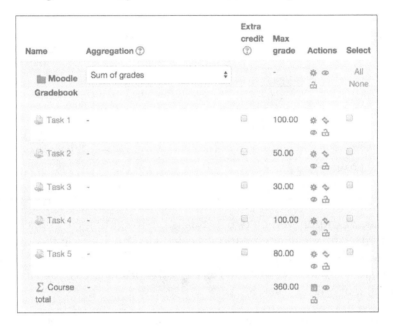

Note the maximum grades for each assessed activity. The maximum grade for the course is the total of each assessed item within the course.

To change the aggregation type, you will use the same process as the one used previously:

1. Go to **Categories and items**.

2. Change the aggregation type to **Sum of grades** and click on **Save changes** at the bottom of the screen.

3. Now, switch back to **View** (**Grader report** in the drop-down list) in the Gradebook.

The calculation for this aggregation is simple. Each graded item is added together and presented as the course total grade. Normalization does not occur, and it is not possible to exclude empty grades (ungraded items). This aggregation simply adds each item to the total as it is graded.

Surname ▲ First name	Email address	Task 1 ⬍	Task 2 ⬍	Task 3 ⬍	Task 4 ⬍	Task 5 ⬍	Σ Course total ⬍
			Moodle Gradebook				
Ava B	AvaB@mail.com	93.00	36.00	-	-	-	129.00
Emilie H	EmilieH@mail.com	97.00	50.00	27.00	-	-	174.00
Bayley W	BayleyW@mail.com	85.00	14.00	-	-	-	99.00
Madeline W	MadelineW@mail.com	89.00	42.00	14.00	-	-	145.00
Overall average		91.00	35.50	20.50	-	-	136.75

However, it is possible to apply some extra credit within this grade type.

Go back to the **Categories and items** page from within the grades area and notice the **Extra credit** column. For each graded item within the course, there is an option for it to be chosen for extra credit. So, what does this do?

Any item that has extra credit applied to it is considered an additional assessment and therefore, the maximum grade is not used in the course total.

For example, the course can have four required tasks. A student might not submit **Task 2** on time or not get a sufficient grade, but they are not allowed to resubmit. **Task 5** could be an additional or alternative task that can be used to increase the final course score. Another use of extra credit could be where the student has completed all work but has the option to improve their final grade by completing additional work.

In the example we are using, the course total is currently 360, which is calculated by adding all the maximum grades of each assessed item together. We are going to set **Task 5** as the extra credit. This will mean that the maximum grade of 80 is not included in the calculation of the course total. Let's apply this; go to the **Categories and items** screen and check the Extra credit column for **Task 5** and click on **Save changes** at the bottom of the screen.

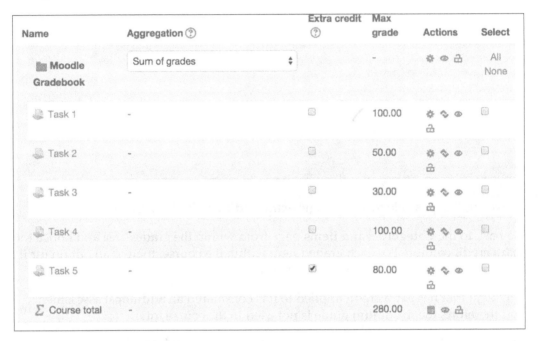

Name	Aggregation ⑦	Extra credit ⑦	Max grade	Actions	Select
📁 **Moodle Gradebook**	Sum of grades ⬍		-	⚙ ⊙ 🔒	All None
📄 Task 1	-	☐	100.00	⚙ ↷ ⊙ 🔒	☐
📄 Task 2	-	☐	50.00	⚙ ↷ ⊙ 🔒	☐
📄 Task 3	-	☐	30.00	⚙ ↷ ⊙ 🔒	☐
📄 Task 4	-	☐	100.00	⚙ ↷ ⊙ 🔒	☐
📄 Task 5	-	☑	80.00	⚙ ↷ ⊙ 🔒	☐
Σ Course total	-		280.00	▦ ⊙ 🔒	

Note that the course total grade is now 280 instead of 360.

The maximum grade that a student can receive will always be 280. For example, if a student receives a grade of 100 in **Task 1**, 50 in **Task 2**, 30 in **Task 3**, 100 in **Task 4**, and also completes **Task 5** and receives a grade of 80, their course total will still say 280. This is because it is not possible to get a grade that is higher than the course maximum. However, the extra credit will mean that students have an additional chance to receive the highest grade possible.

Viewing letter grades in the Gradebook

Until now, we have been viewing the results in the Gradebook as numbers.

In *Chapter 2*, *Customizing Grades*, we created letter grades to show numbers as a corresponding word of our choice rather than the numbers that we used to grade (for example, **Distinction** instead of **100**). We used the following percentages for the grade letters:

Letter grade	Highest percentage	Lowest percentage
Distinction	100%	100%
Merit	99.99%	75%
Pass	74.99%	50%
Not yet complete	49.99%	0%

If you are following these instructions within your own course, then make sure that you have the letter grades set up, as shown in the preceding table. If you cannot remember how to do this, refer to *Chapter 2*, *Customizing Grades*.

We can apply these to our Gradebook so that instead of seeing a final number grade, we will see a word based on the percentage that the learner has received.

This takes some setting up! Take a look:

1. Go to the **Grades** area (navigate to **Administration | Grades**)

2. Go to **Categories and items** (either by clicking on the drop-down list and clicking on **Simple view** under the **categories and items** heading, or by clicking on **Categories and items** on the tabs bar).

3. Click on the edit icon at the top of the **Actions** column (this is usually a cog icon, and it will be next to the category aggregation drop-down list).

4. You need to view the **Category total** options and click on **Show more** to see the settings we need.

5. Look for the **Grade display type** option. It probably says **Default (Real)** in the current setting. Click on the drop-down list and you will see a range of options. There are three main options:

   ° **Letter**: This shows you the relevant letter grade in relation to the percentage setup in the letter grades options.

   ° **Percentage**: This will show you the grade as a percentage. Moodle will calculate the percentage grade based on the grade awarded and the maximum grade possible.

   ° **Real**: This will show you the actual grade awarded in the grading process. This is what is currently displayed as the default.

You might notice that there are actually more than three options available in the drop-down list. You will see that more options are there apart from the ones described in the preceding points. This allows you to choose two grades to be shown within the Gradebook. For example, if **Letter (percentage)** is chosen, the letter will be shown as the main grade in the Gradebook, and the corresponding percentage will be shown in brackets next to it.

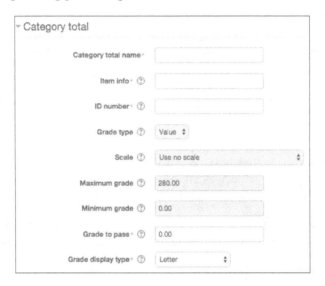

6. From the drop-down list, choose **Letter** and click on **Save changes** at the bottom of the screen.

7. Switch back to **View** (**Grader report** in the drop-down list) in the Gradebook.

Take a look at the course total and note that the **Course total** column now has the words that have been set up as the letter grades. These are shown based on a calculated percentage grade, which is based on the work graded so far.

Surname ▲ First name		Email address	🎯 Task 1 ⇕	🎯 Task 2 ⇕	🎯 Task 3 ⇕	🎯 Task 4 ⇕	🎯 Task 5 ⇕	Σ Course total ⇕
	Ava B	AvaB@mail.com	93.00	36.00	.	-	-	Not yet complete
	Emilie H	EmilieH@mail.com	97.00	50.00	27.00	.	-	Pass
	Bayley W	BayleyW@mail.com	85.00	14.00	.	.	-	Not yet complete
	Madeline W	MadelineW@mail.com	89.00	42.00	14.00	.	-	Pass
		Overall average	91.00	35.50	20.50	-	-	Not yet complete

Moodle Gradebook

You can see that **Ava B** and **Bayley W** have not yet received sufficient grades to gain an actual grade yet (which means that they have received less than a 50 percent grade according to how our letter grades have been set up). As more work is completed and graded, the course total will increase and therefore the final grade will change.

Note that the tasks are still displayed as real number grades. It is possible to change the settings for individual assignments in order to display alternative grade display types as well. Let's go in and change these:

1. Go back to **Categories and items**.

2. This time, click on the edit (cog) icon next to the first graded item on the list (in the example we have been using, this will be **Task 1**).

3. Find the **Grade display type** option (you will need to click on **Show more**) and change it to **Letter**.

4. Click on **Save changes** at the bottom of the screen.

Repeat this process for all the assessed activities in the course (or as many as you want in order to show a letter grade instead of a number grade). Take a look at the grader report again to see the letter grades instead of numbers shown in the Gradebook.

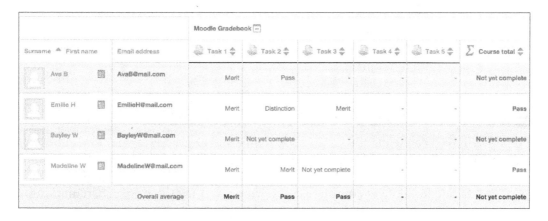

Surname ▲ First name		Email address	🎓 Task 1 ⬍	🎓 Task 2 ⬍	🎓 Task 3 ⬍	🎓 Task 4 ⬍	🎓 Task 5 ⬍	Σ Course total ⬍
Ava B	🖼	AvaB@mail.com	Merit	Pass	-	-	-	Not yet complete
Emilie H	🖼	EmilieH@mail.com	Merit	Distinction	Merit	-	-	Pass
Bayley W	🖼	BayleyW@mail.com	Merit	Not yet complete	-	-	-	Not yet complete
Madeline W	🖼	MadelineW@mail.com	Merit	Merit	Not yet complete	-	-	Pass
		Overall average	**Merit**	**Pass**	**Pass**	-	-	**Not yet complete**

The process to change the way in which the grades are displayed is the same for all types of aggregation and any graded activity. However, it always needs to be completed through the Gradebook for each individual item, so it could be quite time-consuming for courses with lots of graded items.

If the course is going to use the same grade display types, you can set the course default to an alternative (other than **Real**, which is the current default).

Setting the course default for the grade display type

The course default can be set up as follows:

1. Within the **Grades** screen, we need to go to the **Settings** area (if using the drop-down list, find the **Settings** heading and click on **Course**; if using the tabs view, click on **Settings**).

2. Find the **Grade item settings** section and click on the drop-down list to change the **Default (Real)** option to the option you would like for the course. Save the changes on this screen.

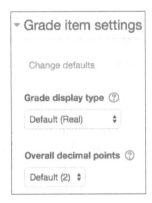

You will still be able to change each assignment type or total to an alternative grade display type, but all future graded activities will be presented as this chosen grade display type within the course.

Example three – using scales

So far, we have been using the Gradebook with number grades (apart from choosing to view these as letter grades). However, courses can also use scales, which are often words used for grading instead of numbers. In *Chapter 2, Customizing Grades* we set up a word scale for **Not yet complete**, **Pass**, **Merit**, and **Distinction**. When marking as assignment, we pick one of these words as the grade.

Remember that scales have a simple scoring system based on the number of items in the scale rather than true numbers. Therefore, they are not always the best option for complex calculations. However, let's use some scales in the Gradebook to see the calculations in action.

For this example, there are five tasks within the course, and each one is graded on the **PMD** scale set up in *Chapter 2, Customizing Grades* (with these options for grading: **Not yet complete**, **Pass**, **Merit**, and **Distinction**).

You can see how these have been graded so far in the following screenshot:

Surname ▲ First name	Email address	📋 Task 1 ⬍	📋 Task 2 ⬍	📋 Task 3 ⬍	📋 Task 4 ⬍	📋 Task 5 ⬍	∑ Course total ⬍
Ava B	AvaB@mail.com	Pass	Pass	-	-	-	4.00
Emilie H	EmilieH@mail.com	Merit	Distinction	Merit	-	-	10.00
Bayley W	BayleyW@mail.com	Merit	Distinction	-	-	-	7.00
Madeline W	MadelineW@mail.com	Distinction	Merit	Distinction	-	-	11.00
Overall average		Merit	Merit	Distinction	-	-	8.00

The course aggregation for this example has been set to **Sum of grades**, and the Gradebook adds together each grade that is awarded in order to show the course total.

Remember, from *Chapter 2, Customizing Grades*, the numbers that are used in calculations when using scales are based on the number of items in the scale. In this four-point scale, the grades will be 1 to 4 (**Not yet complete = 1**, **Pass = 2**, **Merit = 3**, and **Distinction = 4**) as the sum of grades is not a normalized scale.

Take a look at **Emilie H** in the previous screenshot. Her course total is 10. This is calculated in the following way:

3 (Merit) + 4 (Distinction) +3 (Merit) = 10.

Let's change the aggregation type from **Sum of grades** to **Mean of grades** in the **Categories and items** screen. Also, make sure that the course total at the bottom of the screen says **100.00**. If it does not, then change the number and click on **Save changes** at the bottom of the screen. Go back to the **Grader** view to see how the course total has changed.

Surname ▲ First name	Email address	📋 Task 1 ⬍	📋 Task 2 ⬍	📋 Task 3 ⬍	📋 Task 4 ⬍	📋 Task 5 ⬍	$\bar{X}$ Course total ⬍
Ava B	AvaB@mail.com	Pass	Pass	-	-	-	33.33
Emilie H	EmilieH@mail.com	Merit	Distinction	Merit	-	-	77.78
Bayley W	BayleyW@mail.com	Merit	Distinction	-	-	-	63.33
Madeline W	MadelineW@mail.com	Distinction	Merit	Distinction	-	-	88.89
Overall average		Merit	Merit	Distinction	-	-	70.83

Take a look at **Emilie H** again. This aggregation method uses a normalization process, and the calculation is shown in the following table. As we know, the scores used with scales will always be based on the number of items in the scale and the Gradebook will always use either 0 or 1 (depending on the aggregation chosen) for the first item in the scale. When using normalized aggregation, methods scales start from 0, so the four-point scale will have a range from 0 to 3 (0 = **Not yet complete**, 1 = **Pass**, 2 = **Merit**, and 3 = **Distinction**).

	Task 1	Task 2	Task 3	Total	Mean aggregation	The final grade shown in the Gradebook
Maximum grade possible	3 (for distinction)	3	3			
Grade awarded	2 (merit)	3 (distinction)	2 (merit)	7	2.333	
Normalized grade	0.6667 (2/3)	1 (3/3)	0.6667 (2/3)	2.3334 (0.6667 + 1 + 0.6667)	0.7778 (2.3334/3)	77.78 (0.7778*100)

This process will be the same for all normalized methods (with the aggregation calculation relevant to the method chosen).

In these two examples, the course total has been shown as numbers. However, it is possible to set the course total to use the scale as well.

1. Go to the **Categories and items** area in the Gradebook and click on the edit button next to the **Aggregation** drop-down menu.

2. In the **Category total** section, find the **Grade type option** and choose the scale from the list.

3. This will activate the **Scale** drop-down list. From this list, choose the **PMD** scale, which is the same scale used for the individual assessments.

4. Click on the **Show more** text to view the **Grade display type** options.

5. Make sure that the **Grade display type** option says **Real** and **Save changes** at the bottom of the screen.

6. Now, switch back to **View** the **Grader report** option again.

You can see that the course total is now using the same scale as the graded items.

The **Course total** scale uses the same scoring as the individual items and uses the aggregation method to decide which item of the scale is to be displayed.

Take a look at **Emilie H** again. Remember that the normalized total was **2.3334**. As two equates to **Merit** in this four-point scale, **Merit** is shown as the course grade. Remember, this example does not use the nongraded assessments in the total, so the grade will change as other assignments are completed. If the normalized grade is calculated as .5, the final grade will be rounded up. For example, the normalized grade of **Bayley W** will be **2.5** (a grade of 2 for **Merit** and a grade of 3 for **Distinction** to make a total of **5**.) This, divided by two for the number of grades in the mean calculation, provides the **2.5** normalized total. This is rounded up to display a final course grade of **Distinction**.

Example four – using outcomes

We have seen a range of ways in which Moodle can use numbers, letters, and words to calculate the final course total. We will now look at how the outcomes we set in *Chapter 2, Customizing Grades* can be used in the course totals.

In this example, two assignment tasks have been set up with no grade but each has different outcomes applied to them. The outcomes are graded using the completion scale set up in *Chapter 2, Customizing Grades*.

When marking this work, only the outcomes are graded (as either **Not yet complete**, **Partially complete**, or **Complete**). We will need to tell the Gradebook to include outcomes in the grade aggregation.

For this example, students need to ensure that all the assignment outcomes are complete so a lowest grade aggregation will be used. This is useful as all outcomes need to be marked as complete for the course to be complete. If there is one **Not yet complete** or **Partially complete** grade, this will be shown as the course total and therefore, teachers and students will know that some work still needs to be completed. Once all outcomes are graded as complete, the lowest grade will be **Complete** and this will be shown in the **Course total** column. For these elements to be shown in the course total, the **Course total grade type** option needs to be the 'complete' scale. This process requires a running total based on all the required elements, so the aggregation must include nongraded (empty) items in the Gradebook.

There is one new element that needs to be applied here, in addition to settings we have previously used. In the following instructions, only the new step (that is, choosing to include the outcomes in the grade aggregation) will be explained. The other steps will be stated but you will need to use previously learned knowledge (or look back through previous pages) to apply them:

1. Go to the **Categories and items** screen.
2. Change the **Aggregation** type to **Lowest grade**.

3. Click on the edit icon in the **Actions** column, then click on **Show more** in the **Grade category** section, and remove the tick in the box next to **Aggregate only non-empty items**. Also, click on the box to add a tick next to **Include outcomes in aggregation**.

4. In the **Category total** section, ensure that the **Grade type** option is set to **Scale** and choose the **Completion** scale from the drop-down list.

5. Make sure the **Grade display type** option is set to **Real** (we need to click on **Show more** to check this).

6. Scroll to the bottom of the screen and click on **Save changes**.

7. Then, switch to **View** the full **Grader report**.

When using outcomes, the Gradebook screen has a lot more information in it as each outcome is listed as an additional column on the screen. Using lots of outcomes can make the Gradebook a little difficult to use and will require some scrolling on your screen. However, you can see some of the items that have been graded and the course totals in the following screenshot:

No grade will be shown in the main assignment column (**Task 2** in the previous example) as it has been set up with no grade, but it has two outcomes (shown with a circle icon) attached to it, which are are graded with a scale. While work is still being submitted and graded, the course total will remain **Not yet complete**. Once a grade has been awarded to all outcomes, the lowest grade will be the one that is shown as the **course total** option. **Emilie H** has submitted all her work and it has been graded, but there is still at least one element that is only partially completed, which is reflected in her course total. However, we can see that **Madeline W** has completed all her tasks, so her course total shows as **Complete**.

Summary

In this chapter, we saw a range of ways in which the Gradebook can be used to display student grades and calculate final course grades. We saw how numerical grades and scales can be calculated to show a final course grade. We also investigated how the different grading types and aggregation methods can be used.

With many options available within the Gradebook, aggregation types can be quite confusing. However, having worked through the examples, you should now have a better understanding of the key settings related to the calculation of grades within the Gradebook. This should give you an overall understanding of the aggregation types and settings available, and you can also refer to the chapter in the future to apply the settings you need for your course. You can find explanations of each of the category types at `Moodle.org`: `https://docs.moodle.org/27/en/ Category_aggregation`

In *Chapter 6, Organizing the Gradebook Using Categories*, we will see how we can further customize the Gradebook to organize grades into categories.

6
Organizing the Gradebook Using Categories

The Gradebook can be difficult to use due to the amount of information shown within the table, especially in a course that uses a lot of graded activities. Often, the main course screen is arranged by topics in order to organize the content, and we can apply a similar process to the Gradebook through the use of categories to group grades by topic, assessment type, or any other preferred arrangement.

We have seen how we can carry out course calculations based on how we want all the assignments to be added together. However, what if you want one set of assessments to be calculated as a mean of grades and another group of tasks to show the highest grade? What if you don't want some of the grades to be used in the calculations? We can use categories in a range of ways in order to group assessments together, such as by topic or assessment type. We can also use categories to enable some assessments to have a higher weighting than others. In this chapter, we will:

- Create categories and learn how to add graded activities to them
- See how categories can provide a range of aggregation types within one course
- See ways in which we can exclude grades from the final course total

Adding categories

Categories enable you to group graded activities within the Gradebook so that they can be viewed together and provide additional options to calculate final course grades. We will look at how they can be used throughout this chapter but first, we need to add some categories. We need to create the categories using the **Grades** area of the course:

- Go to the **Grades** area and then go to the **Categories and items** screen (if using the drop-down list, you will need to choose **Simple view**).

- At the bottom of the **Categories and items** screen, there is a button that says **Add category**. Click on this and a new screen will appear.

- Give the category a name (such as Unit 1). Note that the options you get when setting up the category are the same as the options we used in *Chapter 5, Using Calculations* to set up how the course should be aggregated. This includes the grade display type as well as the aggregation method. You can choose the same type of aggregation as the course or use one specific aggregation type for this unit.

- In the **Category total** section, you can set a **Maximum grade** option for the category. Category totals will work in exactly the same way as the course total in order to set a maximum grade available. For example, if Unit 1 has three assessments each worth 100 but the maximum for Unit 1 is 100, the maximum grade can be set and the aggregation will take this into account when presenting a final category total. See the upcoming information box for how this affects the course totals.

- Make any further changes you would like to make to the category.

- When you have added at least one category, you get an additional option at the bottom of the screen in order to choose a **Parent category** option. This allows you to choose whether the category will be a main or a subcategory (a subcategory is a category nested within another category). We will look at the use of subcategories later in the chapter.

- Scroll to the bottom of the screen and click on **Save changes**.

 When using categories, the course total is calculated using the category totals instead of the individual assessment grades. The category will complete the selected aggregation when it is created and present a category total. The course total will then use each category total in the aggregation that has been selected for the course total.

If graded activities have already been added to the course, you can use the **Categories and items** screen to move graded activities to the relevant categories. Once categories have been set up, you can choose the relevant category when initially adding the graded activity to the course.

To move the graded activities into categories, check the small **Select** box next to each activity that you want to move (the **Select** column is on the right-hand side of the screen) and at the bottom of the screen, click on **Move selected items to** and choose the category you would like them to be moved to. You can also use the standard move icon in the **Actions** column to move individual items as required, as shown:

You can also move the order of the categories after they have been created using the moving icon:

1. Click on the move icon next the category you want to move (in the **Actions** column). This will temporarily remove the category from the screen.

2. White boxes will appear on the screen in all the places where can move the category to.

3. Click on the space where you would like the category to be.

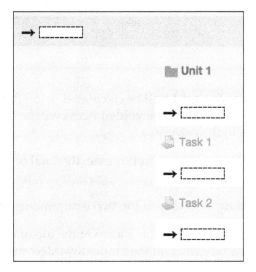

In the following screenshot, you can see that there are three categories within the course and there are two aggregation types used in the course:

For this example, the total of **Unit 1** will be calculated using the 'mean of grades' aggregation type, which means that the graded items will be divided by 2 (the total number of graded items in the category).

Unit 2 will present the sum of grades (in this case, the total of one assignment) as the category total.

Unit 3 will also show a sum of grades of the two assignments as the category total.

The course total will be **Sum of grades** (as shown at the top of the preceding screenshot), which will add together all the grades awarded and shown in the unit category totals. This calculation will be *Unit 1 + Unit 2 + Unit 3*. Individual assessment grades will only be included in the final grade if they are not in a category.

Excluding assessments from the final grade

There might be elements of the online course that are assessed but do not count toward a final grade. These could be formative assessments such as homework activities, quizzes to enable self-assessment, and so on. These graded items will automatically appear in the Gradebook, but you might not want the grades to be counted in the final category or the course total.

There are two main ways in which we can do this. One is to exclude a graded activity for all students and the other is to exclude individual grades for each individual student.

Excluding assessments from the aggregation for all students

There are a few ways in which this can be achieved. One has already been mentioned in *Chapter 5*, *Using Calculations*, when using the weighted mean of grades. There are two further ways in which this can be achieved, and both require the use of categories.

If you would like all the graded items that do not count for the course total to be in one category, you can do the following:

1. Go to the **Grades** area and then go to the **Categories and items** page (if using the drop-down list, choose **Simple view** under the **Categories and items** heading).
2. Scroll to the bottom of the screen and click on **Add category**.
3. Give the category a name (such as `formative assessments` or `not used for final grade`).
4. Make sure the aggregation is not a sum of grades (any other aggregation method is fine).
5. Click on **Show more** within the **Category total** section. Find the **Grade type** section and choose **None**.
6. Scroll to the bottom of the screen and click on **Save changes**.

Any graded activities that are listed in this category will not be included in the course total aggregation.

You can also create the same effect by creating a category with a category total of zero.

If you would like to keep the formative assignment and the summative activities within the same category rather than keep all the formative work in a separate category, a subcategory can be used. This enables the graded items to appear together within the Gradebook, but they are not counted in the course total grade. To achieve this:

1. Go the **Grades** area and then go to the **Categories and items** page.

2. Go to the parent category (where you will be adding the subcategory) by clicking on the edit icon next to the category name.

3. Make sure that there is no tick next to **Aggregate including sub-categories**. It is worth mentioning here that if you are using subcategories and want the grades to be included in the course total, you will need to go into the parent category and check this option.

4. Click on **Save changes** at the bottom of the screen.

5. Scroll to the bottom of the screen and click on **Add category**.

6. Give the category a name (such as `formative assessments` or `not used for final grade`).

7. Make sure the aggregation is not sum of grades (any other aggregation method is fine).

8. Click on **Show more** in the **Category total** section and find the **Grade type** section and choose **None**.

9. At the bottom of the screen, click on the drop-down list next to **Parent category**, and choose the **Parent** category that you created previously.

10. Scroll to the bottom of the screen and click on **Save changes**.

Anything moved into this category will not be included in the course aggregation, but it will enable the assignment to be viewed within the Gradebook with the relevant parent category.

Excluding assessments from the aggregation for individual students

If you only want to exclude some grades for some students, you can do this for each individual student for each graded activity:

1. Go to the **Grades** area to view **Grader report** (navigate to **Administration | Grades**).

2. In the top-right corner, click on **Turn editing on**.

3. Once editing is turned on, the edit icon will appear next to each individual graded item (it doesn't matter whether the work has been graded yet or not).

4. Click on the edit icon next to the activity that you would like to exclude from the aggregation.

5. A screen will appear with an option of **Excluded** as shown in the following screenshot. Click on the box next to this option to add a tick to the box.

6. Scroll to the bottom of the screen to click on **Save changes**.

These methods work with all aggregation types except the sum of grades. The sum of grades will always include all grades in the final aggregation. If you are using **Sum of grades**, a warning appears next to the **Excluded** option, reminding the user about this: **excluding of grades is not compatible with sum aggregation**.

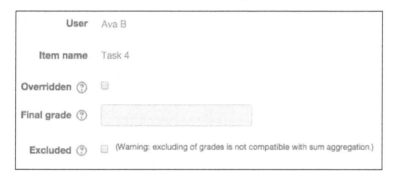

Summary

In this chapter, we saw some ways in which the Gradebook can be organized in order to make it easier to use through the use of categories. Apart from grouping graded items together, categories can also be used to further increase the options for grade calculations by choosing the graded items in a category that will not be included in the final grade. We also saw how to exclude individual grades from the final course total.

In the next chapters, we will look at how we can use the information in the Gradebook to report and review students' achievements.

7
Reporting with the Gradebook

So far, we have seen how we can use number, letter, and scale grades and how we can add assignments to courses. We can grade assignments and set up the Gradebook to calculate course totals.

We will now look at how we can view reports for all students as well as for individual students and some of the other ways in which the grade reports can be customized and exported. There are four main reports:

- The grader report
- The outcomes report
- The overview report
- The user report

The grader report

We have already seen the grader report a few times throughout this book, as it is the main screen we see when we go into the Gradebook.

To get to the grader report, we go to the **Grades** area:

1. Click on **Grades** in the **Administration** block.
2. If you are using the tabs layout, make sure that the **View** tab and **Grader** report are selected. If you are using the drop-down list to navigate the **Grades** area, ensure that the **Grader report** option under the **View** heading is selected.

You can see the tabs and the drop-down menu in the following screenshot:

This report shows you the grades of all the students for each graded activity. This enables the teacher to see the progress of all students in one place.

The report shows you one student per row. For courses with many students, the student rows might appear over two or more pages. In this case, a **Next** button will appear to move to the next page of students. However, we can change how many students are shown per page within the Gradebook preferences. If you have tabs at the top of your screen, click on **Preferences**. If you're using the drop-down list, choose **Grader report** under the **Preferences** heading. Within the **General** section, there is an option to type in how many students per page you would like to view. Click on **Save changes** to save this option.

Within each column, we can see the grade for each assignment. However, with a lot of graded activities in the course, the grader report can be very wide. Categories can be used to organize this content, but the grader report also lets us collapse information to make it even easier to view.

There are three main ways to collapse the information. The following screenshot shows you two rows of grades (for two different students), and there are three categories set up for this course (**Unit 1**, **Unit 2** and **Unit 3**), as shown in the top row. Each category is displayed in a different way.

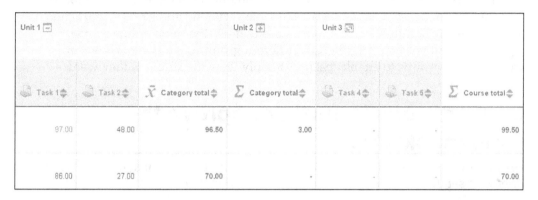

Unit 1 has a – symbol next to it. This is the default way of viewing the category and grade information, and it shows you the full expanded view of grades. It shows you each graded activity within the category (in this case, **Task 1** and **Task 2**) and the **Category total** column.

Unit 2 has a + symbol next to it. This shows you a collapsed view of the category, and only shows you the **Category total** column and not the graded activities that are in that category.

Unit 3 has a square-based symbol next to it, and this shows you the graded activities within the category but not the **Category total** column.

You can click on these symbols next to each category to toggle between each view. The changes are made for the individual user and will be remembered each time the user views the grader report. You can change the way the report is viewed at any time.

 The theme of the Moodle site might show alternative icons to expand and collapse the category views.

A useful option for courses that have a lot of graded activities is to view the **Category total** column only (so that the + symbol is displayed). This will show you all the category totals in the course so that the grader report is not too detailed. The user can then choose to view the full content of the category they are using at that point in time (such as the current unit being delivered).

This is particularly useful for courses where different teachers teach different units, as they can collapse the categories so that they only view the category that they teach.

Another issue with a course that has a lot of content is related to having a lot of students in the course. This can make the table very long and can be a particular issue if there are a number of course groups that use the same online course. Again, different teachers might grade different groups of students. However, we can set up groups to enable teachers to only view the students they want.

Using groups to further improve the Gradebook's use

Groups are a course-wide feature, but this section will give you a quick overview of how to set them up and use them within the Gradebook.

There are three elements that we need to address:

- Creating groups and adding students to groups
- Setting the assignments to enable group views
- Changing the course settings to view groups in the Gradebook

Creating groups

The following steps shows how to create a group in the Gradebook:

1. Go to the main screen of the course and view the **Administration** block. Choose **Users** and click on **Groups**.

2. At the bottom of this screen, click on **Create group**.

3. Type in the name of the group (such as Group A) and click on **Save changes** at the bottom of the screen. Repeat this process for each group required.

4. After the groups have been created, they will appear in the groups list on the left-hand side of the screen. Click on the first group in the list so that it is highlighted and then click on **Add/remove users** in the bottom-right corner of the screen.

5. In the right-hand column on the screen, all current members of the course will appear. Choose the students who should be part of this group by clicking on their name and then clicking on **Add** in the centre of the two columns. Repeat this process for each student.

6. Once the process is complete, click on **Back to groups** at the bottom of the screen. Repeat this process for other groups.

Enabling assignments to use groups

Each assignment that we want to be able to grade in groups has to be set up to enable the use of groups.

This is chosen in the common module settings of the assignment editing screen. This can be done when we initially set up the assignments:

1. When viewing the assignment on the screen, click on **Edit settings** in the **Administration** block.

2. Find the **Common modules settings** section and click on the title to display the options. Find the **Group mode** option and change the option from **No groups** to **Visible groups** or **Separate groups** and **Save and display** the assignment.

3. View the assignment and feedback grading area from within the assignment by clicking on the **View/grade all submissions** text.

4. In the top-left section of the assignment area, you will now see a **Visible groups** or **Separate groups** drop-down list.

You can use this drop-down list to choose the group that you would like to view. This will filter the students and show only the students in the chosen group. You can still view all participants to see all the students on the grading screen.

Viewing the groups in the Gradebook

If we want to view these groups in the grader report, we need to change the course settings:

1. From the main course screen, go to the **Administration** block and click on **Edit settings** under the **Course administration** heading.

2. Scroll down the page and click on the **Groups** option. Change **Group mode** to **Visible groups** or **Separate groups**.

3. Scroll to the bottom of the screen and click on **Save changes**.

4. From the **Administration** block, click on **Grades** to go back to the **Grader report**.

5. You will notice that the **Visible groups** or **Separate groups** drop-down lists are now available at the top of the grader report. Teachers can filter to view groups of students or view all students along with the relevant course grades.

Apart from showing assignment grades for each student, the grader report will also show the outcome grade. However, as the grader report has a lot of information, it can be difficult for the teacher to see whether each outcome is being achieved throughout the whole course. The outcomes report provides a summary of the outcomes used in the course and shows the average outcome grades for the course based on the outcome grades given to date.

Outcomes report

The outcomes report is used in courses where outcomes have been added to the course. Details of how to enable and add outcomes are provided in *Chapter 2, Customizing Grades*. If you have tabs at the top of your screen, click on **View** and then click on the **Outcomes report** under the tabs. If you're using the drop-down list, choose **Outcomes report** under the **View** heading.

The outcomes report can help the teacher see which outcomes are being achieved and at what level; it also helps them see which ones might require additional support or development.

Grader report	Outcomes report	Overview report	User report		
Short name	**Course average**	**Site-wide**	**Activities**	**Average**	**Number of grades**
Evidence provided	Partially complete (2.17)	No	Task 1	Partially complete (2)	4
			Task 2	Partially complete (2.33)	3
Criteria 2 met	Not yet complete (0)	No	-	-	0
Criteria 1 met	Partially complete (2.5)	No	Task 1	Partially complete (2)	4
			Task 2	Complete (3)	3

This previous report lists the three outcomes that have been used within this course. These are shown in the first column with the **Short name** title.

The second column shows you the average grade for each outcome. This average is based on the grades awarded for the outcome divided by the number of times this outcome has been graded. The average is shown in the same scale, as the outcome is graded but the number in brackets is the equivalent number value. Remember that the numbers used by scales are based on the number of items in the scale. In this example, there are three options in the scale (**Not yet complete**, **Partially complete**, and **Complete**), which means that the maximum number will be three. The average for **Evidence provided** is **2.17** and therefore, it will display the **Partially complete** scale value as this is item number two in the scale list.

The **Site-wide** column will state **Yes** or **No**, depending on whether the outcome is used in this course only (in which case, it will say **No**) or whether the outcomes are used throughout the Moodle site (in which case, it will say **Yes**).

The final three columns provide additional details for how the outcomes are used. The **Activities** column shows you each activity that has this outcome assigned. The **Average** column will show you the average grade for the task, and the final **Number of grades** column shows you how many grades this average is based on.

Overview report

The next report that is available is the overview report. (If you have tabs at the top of your screen, click on **View** and then click on the **Overview report** under the tabs. If you're using the drop-down list, choose **Overview report** under the **View** heading.) This can be accessed from any course, but it enables a teacher to view the current course totals of each student for all the courses in which they are currently enrolled on Moodle.

After clicking on **Overview report**, a list of courses will appear, but the first step is to choose a user or student for whom we want to see the current course results. This drop-down list appears on the right-hand side next to **Select a user**.

Once a user has been chosen, the course list will change and display all the courses that the chosen student is enrolled in, and the grade column will show the current grade awarded for each course.

Course name	Grade
MathsGCSE	B2
FS_English_L2	77 (Pass)
L1 InternetSafety	83.00
AS_Psychology	D (4)

The current grade shows the same grade that appears in the **Course total** column of the grader report for each individual course. This grade is likely to change throughout the duration of the course.

The overview report enables teachers to view students' progress across a number of Moodle courses without having to visit each course individually. However, the teacher can choose to review the details of an individual student's progress by clicking on the **Course name** option in the overview list. This will show you the user report of the learner for the chosen course.

User report

You can access the user report in the same way as the grader and overview reports. If you're using the drop-down list, find the **View** heading and click on **User report**. If you're using the tabs menu, click on **View**, and then click on **User report**, which is shown under the tabs.

Like the overview report, the user report requires the teacher to choose a user from the drop-down list on the right-hand side (unless the user report is accessed via the overview report or by clicking on the grades icon next to the student's name in the grader report).

The user report will show you each graded activity in the course along with the current grade awarded for each activity and the feedback given. This has the same information as the grader report, but this information is for an individual student. It also presents the information in a portrait rather than landscape format (the following screenshot only has a few activities within the Gradebook, but for courses with a lot of graded activities, the page will be longer).

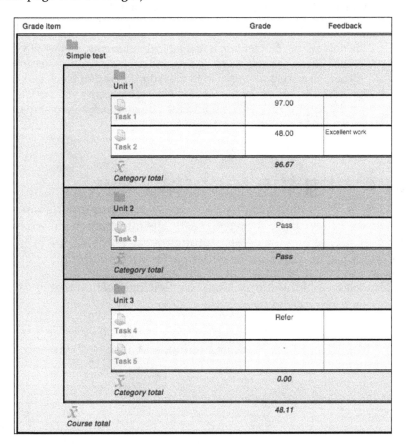

The user report shows you each graded activity from the course in the **Grade item** column with the current **Grade** value awarded next to it. Finally, the **Feedback** column shows you any written feedback given for the activity. If we click on the name of the activity, we can access the full assessment information.

The final row of the column shows you the **Course total** grade so far. This is the same information as what is shown in the **Course total** column in the grader report and in the overview report. In the previous screenshot, this is **48.11**.

Reports that students see

A student can access the Gradebook in the same way as a teacher. They will click on **Grades** in the **Administration** block.

When a student views their grades, it is their own user report that they will see. Students can also view the overview report. Both reports look the same for the students as they do for the teacher. However, they can only see their own reports, whereas a teacher can view the reports for all students in the course.

 By default, the Gradebook is available for students to view. If you would like to turn off access to the grades for students, you can do this in the course settings. Go to the **Administration** block and click on **Edit settings** under the **Course Administration** heading. Click on the **Appearance** title and find the **Show gradebook to students** option and change it from **Yes** to **No**.

Customizing the reports view

We have seen how the grader, outcomes, overview, and user reports can be used and the information that can be shown on each. The information shown in the screenshots used is based on the default settings of each report. However, each of the reports can also be customized to change the information shown.

Within the **Grades** area of the course, there is a **Settings** section that can be used to change how each report is viewed in the course.

This is accessed through the **Settings** tab (if using the tabs layout) or by clicking on the drop-down list. Find the **Settings** heading and click on **Course** (if using the drop-down list option).

A range of options are available for each report type, as shown in the following screenshot:

Change the settings to meet your needs and click on **Save changes** at the bottom of the screen. These settings will be applied to the course rather than the individual user.

> Try changing the settings to see how they can customize your Gradebook and meet your needs.

Exporting the Gradebook data

Apart from viewing the data within Moodle, it is possible to export the Gradebook data and download it to view and use offline. There are four options that are available to download it:

- An OpenDocument spreadsheet
- A plain text file
- An Excel spreadsheet
- An XML file

You access these options from the **Grades** area in Moodle in the same way as you access the reports. How you access the export options will depend on whether you are using the drop-down menu or tab navigation within the **Grades** area. Both options are shown in the following screenshot. If you're using the drop-down menu, find the **Export** heading and click on **OpenDocument spreadsheet** (you can also choose other export options from here). If you're using the tabs layout, click on the **Export** tab. Within the export tab, a second row of options appears, which provides you with the export options.

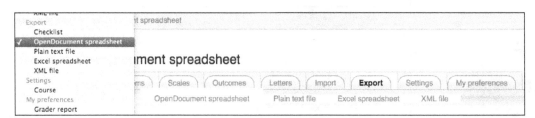

Once you are on the export screen, a range of options are available for you to choose the information to be exported and downloaded.

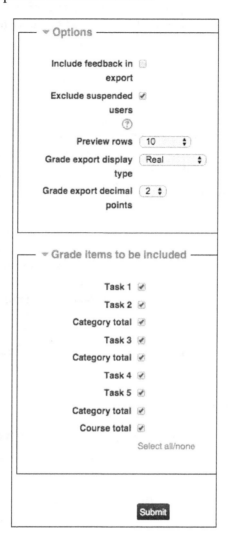

These options are explained as follows:

- **Include feedback in export**: This includes the written feedback alongside the exported data. To include this, we need to click on the box to add a tick.

- **Exclude suspended users**: This is chosen as the default so that only active students are in the exported report. However, if you have any users in the course who have been assigned as suspended but require the data, we will need to remove this tick.

- **Preview rows**: This allows us to choose the number of rows of student data that will be shown once the options are submitted. This allows the teacher to check the data to ensure that it displays the information required before finally exporting the information.

- **Grade export display type**: With this, the teacher can choose whether the real, percentage, or letter grade is the grade shown in the exported data and how many decimal points are shown with the **Grade export decimal points** option.

- **Grade items to be included**: With this, the second part of the options will display all the graded activities, category totals, and the course totals that are included in the online course. The teacher can choose which elements they would like in the exported data. For example, a teacher might only want to export the data for their own unit. A tick in the box will indicate that the data is to be exported. All items will be ticked by default. Clicking on the tick will remove the tick and therefore, will not include the data in the export.

- Click on **Submit** to start the export process.

After clicking on **Submit**, a preview screen will appear with a **Download** button on it.

Preview rows

First name	Surname	ID number	Institution	Department	Email address	Assignment: Task 1	Assignment: Task 2	Assignment: Task 3	Attendance grade	Course total
Ava	B				AvaB@mail.com	-	-	-	-	-
Emilie	H				EmilieH@mail.com	-	-	80.00	-	80.00
Bayley	W				BayleyW@mail.com	Pass	-	-	-	66.04
Madeline	W				MadelineW@mail.com	-	12.00	-	-	60.00

The **Download** button will download the chosen Gradebook data in the selected format.

Summary

In this chapter, we saw the range of ways in which the Gradebook can be used and customized to display the data required for both teachers and students.

Teachers can see all student grades and individual user data as well as set up groups to aid the marking and review process. Students and teachers can also see an overview of all the courses that a user is enrolled on to see the current final grade for each course.

These reports provide the main options to view grades. However, there are a few further customizations that can aid the progress tracking. The final chapter will outline some of these options to further enable the tracking of students' progress.

8
Additional Features for Progress Tracking

The Gradebook is a very useful tool to manage the progress of students. It enables teachers to review and manage the grades awarded for each graded activity in the course. However, there are also some other functions within Moodle that enable the Gradebook to be further enhanced or to track progress outside it. In this chapter we will do the following:

- Set pass grades to visually show achievement and progression for individual pieces of work
- Turn on activity tracking to show progress through activities on the course
- Use course completion to track progress through required elements of the course
- Use course and activity completion reports

Setting pass grades

As we know, we can view the grades awarded in the Gradebook. However, we can also set pass levels for each graded activity to provide a visual view within the Gradebook. When pass grades are set, the Gradebook will not only show the grade but a text color will also be applied. If the grade awarded is below the pass grade, the text color will be red. If the grade awarded is at or above the pass grade, the text color will be green.

This option is set from within the Gradebook and needs to be set for each individual activity.

1. Go into the Gradebook by clicking on **Grades** in the **Administration** block.

2. Go into the **Simple view** option of the **Categories and items** section of the Gradebook.

 You can also complete these tasks by turning editing on within the grader report and clicking on the edit icon next to the graded item.

3. Click on the edit icon (a cog in the **Actions** column) next to the graded item for which you would like to set the pass grade.

4. Click on **Show more** in the **Grade item** section.

5. You will see the **Maximum grade** option that was set when the activity was first created, along with the **Minimum grade** option. Beneath these two options there is the **Grade to pass** setting. By default the grade to pass is **0** but in the following example the pass grade has been set as **95.00**.

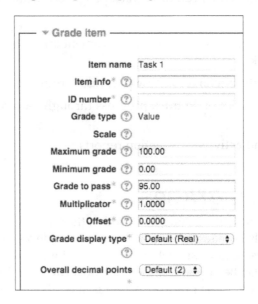

6. Click on **Save changes** at the bottom of the screen.

Once you have saved the grade to pass, return to the **Grader report** option. You will now notice that the text color changes for any grades that have been awarded for this assignment.

On the following screenshot, the grade for **Task 1** for **Madeline W** is shown in green which indicates that it is at or above the required pass grade. However, the grade for **Bayley W** is below the pass grade so the grade is shown in red.

Surname ▼ First name	Email address	📋 Task 1 ⬍	📋 Task 2 ⬍
👤 Madeline W 📰	MadelineW@mail.com	97.00	48.00
👤 Bayley W 📰	BayleyW@mail.com	86.00	27.00

Adding pass grades, where relevant, can help the teacher to quickly see how learners are progressing while viewing the Gradebook. Setting pass grades can also be useful in other areas of Moodle to show a quick summary of whether students have passed or not. For example, setting a pass grade can show whether a task is complete or not when using the activity completion functions.

Activity completion

Activity completion in Moodle allows students and teachers to track the use of resources and activities. This information can be shown to students on the Moodle screen and in a report for teachers. It can also be used as one of the criteria for determining course completion status.

Activity completion can be set for any resource or activity within a course. Each item within the course needs to be set to enable activity completion, so we are able to choose for some items to be tracked while others are not. For the purpose of this chapter, we're only going to set assignments to be tracked, but the instructions are the same for all resources and activities.

In order for activity completion to be used, it needs to be turned on in site administration and course administration.

 Site administrators can find the option by navigating to **Site administration | Advanced features** and they need to tick the **Enable completion tracking** box.

Once **Completion tracking** is turned on for the Moodle site, teachers can turn on the option within the course by going into the **Administration** block and clicking on **Edit settings** under the **Course administration** heading. Once in this screen, we need to scroll down and click on the **Completion tracking** title. Under the **Enable completion tracking** field, change the option to **Yes** to turn on this option:

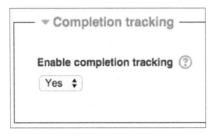

Click on **Save changes** at the bottom of the screen. We can now add activity tracking to any resource or activity within the course. We have already set the option for a pass grade on an assignment, so we will now also add activity completion to it to see how this enables us to check progress.

1. View the assignment on the screen and click on **Edit settings** in the **Administration** block.

2. Scroll down and click on the **Activity completion** text toward the bottom of the page:

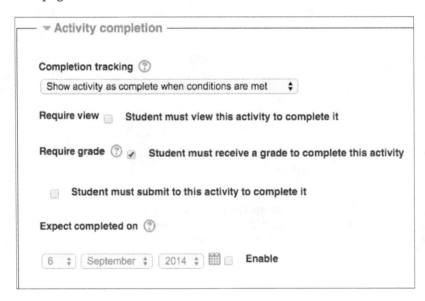

3. The **Completion tracking** drop-down list will have three options:

    °   **Do not indicate activity completion**: The resource will appear on the Moodle course without any activity completion options.

    °   **Students can manually mark as complete**: Students will tick the activity to show that they have viewed or completed it. This is often a good choice for Moodle resources where you want to track whether the student has read the content. For example, the student ticks the activity to say they have read it as Moodle can only tell if a student has clicked on the link.

    °   **Show activity as complete when conditions are met**: Moodle will indicate whether the resource or activity has been completed or not. Depending on the type of activity, the options for completion vary. This is often the best option to choose for Moodle activities where specific tasks need to be completed.

4. Choose **Show activity as complete when conditions are met**.

5. The options below the drop-down list are the different ways in which Moodle can decide whether the activity has been completed or not and will vary depending on the type of activity. All resources and activities will have the **Student must view this activity to complete it** option. However, since an assignment is a graded activity, we also get the **Student must receive a grade to complete this activity** option. Put in a tick in the box to choose this option.

6. Scroll to the bottom of the screen and click on **Save and return to course**.

Take a look at the course screen and you will now notice a tick box icon on the right-hand side of the assignment:

The box indicates that the resource has activity completion settings associated with it, and a tick will appear in the box when the activity is complete. This icon is viewed by individual students to show their progress through the course.

The tick box shown in the previous screenshot has a dotted outline. This indicates that Moodle will be adding the tick when the activity is complete. For activities where the student will mark the activity as complete, this box is shown with a solid line. Students will add a tick on the box to state that the activity has been completed. A good tip is to add instructions into the description box when setting up the activity to tell the students that they will need to click inside the box to mark the activity as complete.

By default, as soon as the assignment is graded, the activity will be marked as complete. However, as we have set a grade to pass, the activity will be marked as complete only when the assignment is graded at or above the required pass grade.

Reporting

Let's take a look at how students and teachers view the activity completion information.

The student view

Students view their progress through the main course screen. Next to each item that has activity completion set up, the student will see a tick once that item has been completed. In the case of assignments with a pass grade, the student will see a tick when the assignment has been graded at the pass grade or higher. If the student does not gain the minimum grade to pass, a cross will appear next to the resource.

The following screenshot shows **Task 1** on the main course screen when **Madeline W** is logged in:

A green tick is shown next to **Task 1**, which means Madeline has completed this task and has achieved at least the minimum pass grade. We can also see that **Task 2** is complete. This is shown with a blue tick and a solid outline on the check box as this has been marked as complete by the student. **Task 3**, **Task 4**, and **Task 5** are not yet complete as they do not have any ticks next to them. This means that either Madeline has not completed the work or the work has not yet been graded.

In the following screenshot, we can see that the course screen of **Bayley W** shows **Task 1** with a red cross next to it to indicate that the assignment has been graded but it has not yet met the required pass grade. This shows that the activity is not yet complete.

The individual course screen and completion status of each activity will vary for each student. However, the teacher will want to see all of the completion information on one screen.

The teacher view

A teacher can view the students' progress through the **Activity completion** report which will show the activity completion status for each student of the course for each activity that has activity completion turned on. To get to this report, we need to use the **Administration** block and find the **Reports** link:

The report we need to use is **Activity completion**. After clicking on this option, we will see a screen similar to the following:

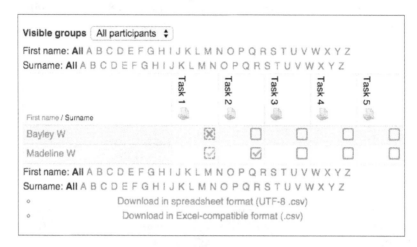

There are many resources within the course but this report will show only those resources and activities where activity completion has been set. We can see each student on the course listed on the left-hand side, and the activities that have activity completion settings added to them will appear across the top of the screen. This table will show the current completion status for each student and for each activity.

In the previous screenshot, we can see that one student has currently passed **Task 1** and one student has not yet passed. If the assignment had not yet been submitted for any student or it hadn't been graded, there would be no color icon in the activity column as shown for **Bayley W** for **Task 2**. Cross icons appear only when grades to pass have been set and the student has not achieved the required grade.

This activity report enables the teacher to very quickly see progress on required items in the course. When used with the **Grade to pass** option, the teacher can very easily view how individual students are progressing in a simple format. It does not, however, provide the specific grade for each assignment, so it does not completely replace the Gradebook. We can click on the activity name in the top row and this will take us to the activity (and give access to the grades) if required. However, in courses where students only need to complete and pass specific activities, the activity completion report could be used instead of the Gradebook for progress tracking.

You will notice that it is possible to choose letters for **First name** and **Surname** to filter the group to see specific students. If you have set up groups in the course as explained in *Chapter 7, Reporting with the Gradebook*, the list of groups will also appear in this activity completion report to filter groups of students. You can also download this data in a spreadsheet for further use and manipulation.

If courses have lots of resources with activity completion added, this report can be quite big. However, it is possible to further select activities for reporting through the use of course completion.

Course completion

Course completion enables the teacher to set the required elements that must be completed in order to achieve the course. This can be used in the same way as activity completion, and it can also be used to complement it.

For example, an online course can contain a wide range of resources and activities that could be a mixture of required elements alongside further supplementary resources. However, some of these activities, such as the assessed elements, might need to be tracked separately by the teacher and looking through the whole activity report could be quite time consuming. This is where course completion can be used.

Within the course, where course completion is to be added, click on the **Administration** block and click on **Course Completion**:

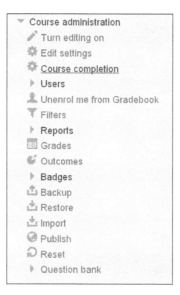

 This needs to be enabled within the course first as explained in the *Activity tracking* section of this chapter.

We have a number of options within the **Completion completion** screen. We can enable one or many options and choose whether all of these options are required or the course will be complete if any one of them has been achieved. These options are as follows:

- **General**: This is where we can choose whether all the options that we set are required or if any of them can be completed (in which case, as long as one of them is completed, the student will complete the course).

- **Condition: Activity completion**: All resources and activities that have activity completion added to them will appear in a list here with a checkbox next to them. It is here that we will choose the required elements that need to be achieved in order to complete the course. For our example, there is a list of all the assignments within the course. Put a tick next to each assignment in your course. At the bottom of the list, there is also an option for you to choose whether students need to complete all or any of these activities. You can see these options in the following screenshot:

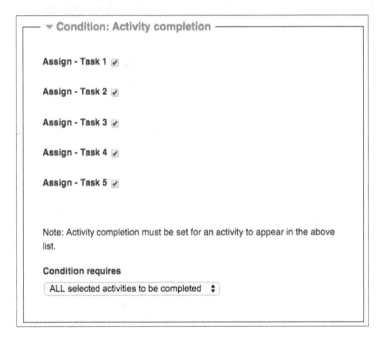

- **Condition: Completion of other courses**: If other courses on the site have course completion set up, we can choose other courses that need to be completed before this course can be marked as complete. Students can work on the online courses concurrently but the course where this setting is enabled will not be marked as complete until the chosen prerequisite courses are also marked as complete. We also get an "any or all" option again.

- **Condition: Date**: If this option is enabled students will not be able to complete the course until at least the date set.

- **Condition: Enrolment duration**: This is similar to the date option but instead of specifying a date, we can choose a length of time that the student needs to be enrolled on the course. If enabled, students will not be able to complete the course until at least the specified number of days from which they became members of the online course.

- **Condition: Unenrolment**: This will mark the course as complete when a student is unenrolled from the course.

- **Condition: Course Grade**: If enabled, a course pass grade can be set. Once the Gradebook course total meets this grade for a student, this element will be marked as complete on the course completion report.

- **Manual self completion**: If this option is enabled, students will be able to indicate that they have completed the course. If we use this option, the self-completion block must also be added to the course to give students the option to choose **Complete course**.

- **Manual completion by**: This can be used as a final checking procedure. If a role is chosen here, any user with that role will need to check all the activities and manually confirm that the work is completed. This is very useful where additional paperwork or checking is required. We also get an "any or all" option here to choose whether multiple roles need to sign off the completion or only one is required. For our example, choose **Teacher**.

- Click on **Save changes**.

Reporting

It is possible to access the course completion report through the **Reports** option within the **Administration** menu in the same way as the activity completion report. However, there is also a block available to further enhance the use of course completion.

To add the block, do the following steps:

1. Click on **Turn editing on**.
2. Find the **Add a block** option (usually at the bottom of all the existing blocks on the left-hand side of the course) and click on **Add**.
3. Choose **Course completion status**.

The teacher view

The block will look like this to the teacher:

You are currently not being
tracked by completion in
this course

View course report

Click on **View course report**. You will see a report similar to the activity completion report but it will only show the options, resources, and activities that were chosen in the course completion setup process:

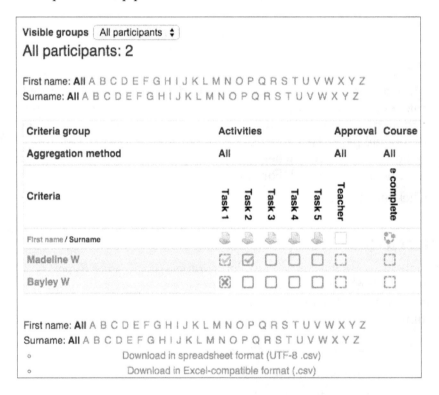

The report shows ticks for **Activities** that have been completed successfully or crosses where a student has not yet met the specific requirements for the activity and has not been awarded the required pass grade (when a **Grade to pass** has been set). There will be no icon shown for the activities that are not yet complete. Note that under the **Activities** title it says **All** indicating that all the activities are required.

Under the **Approval** heading, there is a **Teacher** column. This is used by the teacher to manually tick when they are satisfied that all the required elements have been completed. If no role is set up for manual completion, this column will not be in the course report. If multiple roles had been set up, they would all appear here. Notice again that it shows the **All the approval roles are required** message. In this case, only one is required.

If self-completion has been turned on, this will also be shown here.

Finally, the **Course** heading has a **Course complete** column. When all the required elements have a tick within them, a tick will automatically appear in this column.

 If any course prerequisites or course grades have been set in the **Completion completion** screen, these elements will be shown in the report.

As with the activity completion report, you can view specific students, download the report, and use groups on this screen.

The student view

A student will see a different version of this report and, of course, it will only show them their own data. Let's take a look at what Madeline W would see.

On the main screen of the course, Madeline sees a summary of her progress to date in the **Course completion** status block:

Madeline can see that the course is currently in progress and that two out of the five required activities are complete. Madeline can get further information by clicking on **More details**. This will show the following window:

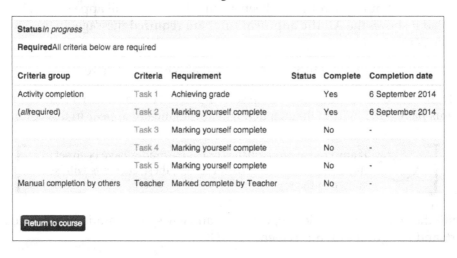

This provides further information about the activities that need to be completed and the current status of each item required. If the activities are complete, the completion date is shown.

If self-completion is enabled for the course, students will also see a **Self completion** option within this report. When using this option, the **Self completion** block must also be added to the course. This block contains a link that says **Complete course**. This is clicked when the student is ready to complete the course (that is, when they feel that everything is finished and complete):

After clicking on the **Complete course** text, the student will be asked to confirm by clicking on **Yes** or **No**:

Please note that students can click on this even if the required course activities are not yet complete.

 The activity and course completion reports are updated when the cron job is completed on the server. This captures the most up-to-date information in relation to Moodle activities to ensure the reports are up to date. If the reports need to be constantly up to date, the cron job might need to be set up to run regularly. Speak with your Moodle administrator to find out more about the cron job.

Summary

These activity and course completion options can be used to complement the Gradebook or in courses where the Gradebook itself may be too complex to review. They can also be used to show a simpler view of the elements that the student has achieved to date. The teacher can choose the specific resources and activities that they want to be able to report on regularly, and yet use the Gradebook for additional detail. In addition, we have seen how course completion settings can be used to monitor the completion of essential elements within a course.

This book has shown some of the key ways in which the Gradebook can be used to manage learning and monitor progress through a course for both teachers and students. The Gradebook is a complex and sophisticated tool and has some further advanced functions for calculating final grades. However, the preset options still provide a wide range of functions and we have explored a range of ways in which the Gradebook can be customized to meet specific needs.

I really hope that you have found this book useful and, more importantly, identified some potential uses for your online courses that you can apply to aid your day to day management of online learning.

Keep experimenting, playing, and trying new ideas, but most of all, happy Moodling!

Index

N

normalization
  need for 75, 76
number grade
  online assignment, creating with 30, 31
  online text assignment,
      grading with 62-65
numerical grade 11
numeric grades 13, 14

O

online assignment
  creating, with number grade 30, 31
online text assignment
  grading, with number grade 62-65
outcomes
  about 21
  assignment, grading with 65-67
  using 22, 23, 100, 101
outcomes report 117, 118
overview report 118

P

pass grades
  setting 127, 128

Q

Quick grading option, assignment
      grading screen 61, 62
Quick grading option, within
      Gradebook 73, 74

R

reports view
  customizing 120-122
rubrics method
  about 39-44
  assignment, grading with 70, 71

S

scale
  about 11-13
  assignment, creating with 26-29
  creating, for assignments grading 18, 19
  examples 18
  using 96-99
Separate and connected ways of
      knowing option
  about 13
  URL 13
simple weighted mean of grades 77, 85, 86
Standard scales 13
students
  reports, viewing 120
student view, activity completion
      report 132, 133
student view, course completion
      report 139-141
Submission settings section, assignment
  Attempts reopened drop-down list 29
  Maximum attempts 29
  Require students click submit button 28
  Require that students accept the submission
      statement 28
sum of grades
  about 78
  example 90-92

T

teacher view, activity completion
      report 133-135
teacher view, course completion
      report 138, 139

U

Use marking workflow feature 29
user report 119, 120

W

weighted mean of grades 76, 87-89

Thank you for buying
Moodle Gradebook
Second Edition

About Packt Publishing

Packt, pronounced 'packed', published its first book, *Mastering phpMyAdmin for Effective MySQL Management*, in April 2004, and subsequently continued to specialize in publishing highly focused books on specific technologies and solutions.

Our books and publications share the experiences of your fellow IT professionals in adapting and customizing today's systems, applications, and frameworks. Our solution-based books give you the knowledge and power to customize the software and technologies you're using to get the job done. Packt books are more specific and less general than the IT books you have seen in the past. Our unique business model allows us to bring you more focused information, giving you more of what you need to know, and less of what you don't.

Packt is a modern yet unique publishing company that focuses on producing quality, cutting-edge books for communities of developers, administrators, and newbies alike. For more information, please visit our website at www.packtpub.com.

About Packt Open Source

In 2010, Packt launched two new brands, Packt Open Source and Packt Enterprise, in order to continue its focus on specialization. This book is part of the Packt Open Source brand, home to books published on software built around open source licenses, and offering information to anybody from advanced developers to budding web designers. The Open Source brand also runs Packt's Open Source Royalty Scheme, by which Packt gives a royalty to each open source project about whose software a book is sold.

Writing for Packt

We welcome all inquiries from people who are interested in authoring. Book proposals should be sent to author@packtpub.com. If your book idea is still at an early stage and you would like to discuss it first before writing a formal book proposal, then please contact us; one of our commissioning editors will get in touch with you.

We're not just looking for published authors; if you have strong technical skills but no writing experience, our experienced editors can help you develop a writing career, or simply get some additional reward for your expertise.

Moodle 2.5 Multimedia Cookbook

Second Edition

ISBN: 978-1-78328-937-0   Paperback: 300 pages

75 recipes to help you integrate different multimedia resources into your Moodle courses to make them more interactive

1. Add all sorts of multimedia features to your Moodle course.

2. Lots of easy-to-follow, step-by-step recipes.

3. Work with sound, audio, and animation to make your course even more interactive.

Moodle for Mobile Learning

ISBN: 978-1-78216-438-8   Paperback: 234 pages

Connect, communicate, and promote collaboration with your coursework using Moodle

1. Adopts practical ideas for demonstrating how to implement mobile learning with Moodle.

2. Empowers you to apply mobile learning in your profession.

3. Discover how other organizations have successfully achieved mobile learning.

4. Filled with practical and hands-on tutorials for learning practitioners.

Please check **www.PacktPub.com** for information on our titles

Moodle JavaScript Cookbook

ISBN: 978-1-84951-190-2   Paperback: 180 pages

Over 50 recipes for making your Moodle system more
dynamic and responsive with JavaScript

1. Learn why, where, and how to add
   JavaScript to your Moodle site.

2. Get the most out of Moodle's built-in
   extra — the Yahoo! User Interface
   Library (YUI).

3. Explore a wide range of modern interactive
   features, from AJAX to animation.

4. Integrate external libraries such as jQuery
   framework with Moodle.

Moodle Gradebook

ISBN: 978-1-84951-814-7   Paperback: 128 pages

Set up and customize the gradebook to track student
progress through Moodle

1. Use Moodle's powerful Gradebook more
   effectively to monitor and report on the
   progress of your students.

2. Customize the Gradebook to calculate and
   show the information you need.

3. Discover new grading features and tracking
   functions that are now available in Moodle 2.

Please check **www.PacktPub.com** for information on our titles

www.ingramcontent.com/pod-product-compliance
Lightning Source LLC
Chambersburg PA
CBHW060142060326
40690CB00018B/3957